Reading Study Guide

McDougal Littell

World History

Medieval and
Early Modern Times

McDougal Littell
A HOUGHTON MIFFLIN COMPANY

Evanston, Illinois • Boston • Dallas

Printed in the United States of America.

ISBN-13: 978-0-618-53075-5   ISBN-10: 0-618-53075-4

7 8 9 -VHE-10 09 08 07

Reading Study Guide

Contents

How to Use This *Reading Study Guide*

The purpose of this *Reading Study Guide* is to help you read and understand your history textbook, *World History: Medieval and Early Times*. You can use this *Reading Study Guide* in two ways.

1. Use the *Reading Study Guide* side-by-side with your history book.

    • Turn to the lesson that you are going to read in the textbook. Then, next to the book, put the pages from the *Reading Study Guide* that accompany that lesson. All of the heads in the *Reading Study Guide* match the heads in the textbook.

    • Use the *Reading Study Guide* to help you read and organize the information in the textbook.

Strategy: Read the Terms & Names and the definition of each. The Terms & Names are in dark type in the section.

Try This: What are the definitions of "Byzantine Empire" and "schism"?

Strategy: Fill in the diagram as you read. The diagram will help you organize information in the lesson.

Try This: What is the purpose of this diagram?

Name

CHAPTER 2 | LESSON 3 The Early Byzantine Empire

Lesson 3 The Early Byzantine Empire

BEFORE YOU READ

In the last section, you read how the Roman Empire split into east and West. The western part fell to invaders. In this lesson you will learn how the eastern half became the Byzantine Empire.

AS YOU READ

As you read Lesson 3, use a chart like the one below to list the main causes and effects of the split in Christianity.

Causes	Effects

TERMS & NAMES

• **Byzantine Empire** the eastern half of the former Roman Empire
• **Justinian I** powerful ruler of the Byzantine Empire
• **Justinian Code** a legal code that organized much of Byzantine life
• **schism** an official split of Christianity that led to two new Christian churches
• **Roman Catholic** Christian church in the West
• **Orthodox** Christian church in the East

CHAPTER 2

Justinian Builds a New Rome
(pages 59–60)
What were the main characteristics of the Byzantine Empire?
In 476, the Western Roman Empire fell. The eastern half of the empire survived and became known as the **Byzantine Empire.** The empire soon became strong and powerful. This was due in large part to the efforts of one the empire's early rulers **Justinian I.**

Justinian ruled from 527 to 565. He expanded the empire and recaptured some of the land Roman rulers had lost. He also developed a law code known as the **Justinian Code.** The code regulated much of Byzantine life and served the empire for 900 years. Justinian also undertook many large public works and building projects including the

rebuilding of a famous church, the Hagia Sophia. Justinian was aided in his efforts by his wife and trusted advisor, Theodora.

1. What were some of Justinian's main achievements?

_____

_____

_____

Copyright © by McDougal Littell, a division of Houghton Mifflin Company

Chapter 2, Lesson 3 **19**
Reading Study Guide

Strategy: Read the summary. It contains the main ideas and the key information under the head.

Try This: What do you think this section will be about?

---

2. Use the *Reading Study Guide* to study for tests on the textbook.

• Reread the summary of every chapter.

• Review the definitions of the Terms & Names in the *Reading Study Guide*.

• Review the diagram of information that you filled out as you read the summaries.

• Review your answers to questions.

READING STUDY GUIDE CONTINUED

The Rise of Constantinople

(page 60)

What was life like in Constantinople?

Constantinople was the capital of the Byzantine Empire. Its location between Europe and southwest helped it to become a center of business and trade.

Merchant stalls lined the street and sold products from distant corners of Asia, Africa, and Europe. The citizens of Constantinople could enjoy many attractions, including numerous activities at the city's large arena, the Hippodrome.

2. How did Constantinople's location affect its growth?

_____

_____

_____

Disagreements Split Christianity

(pages 61–63)

What two churches emerged from the split in Christianity?

Because of its location between Europe and Asia, ideas from both areas influenced the Byzantine Empire. The Byzantine Empire developed a unique culture. For example, Christianity developed differently in the Byzantine Empire than it did in the West.

In the West, Christianity had a well-organized structure with priests, bishops, and the pope as the leader of the entire Christian Church.

As the Byzantine Empire grew, popes and Byzantine emperors often disagreed. Both felt they should have the final say in religious matters. The two sides become involved in a major conflict over the use of icons. These are religious images that many Eastern Christians used to aid their prayers. In 730, the Byzantine Emperor Leo III banned the use of icons. He viewed them as idol worship, or the belief in false gods. The pope favored the use of icons. He excommunicated, or removed from the church, the Byzantine emperor.

Further conflicts between Christian leaders in the East and West led to a **schism**, or official split, in 1054. This split resulted in the creation of two new churches: the **Roman Catholic** Church in the West and the **Orthodox** Church in the East.

The two churches were alike in some ways, but were organized differently. Each also followed beliefs that set them apart. For example, each group viewed relations between the church and the state differently. In the Roman Catholic Church, the pope claimed authority over kings and emperors as well as the church. In the Eastern Orthodox Church, the emperor ruled over the patriarch, the religious leader of the Orthodox Church.

3. How did the schism of 1054 affect Christianity?

_____

_____

_____

_____

Strategy: Underline main ideas and key information as you read.

Try This: read the summary under the head "Disagreements Split Christianity." Underline information that you think is important.

Strategy: Answer the question at the end of each part.

Try This: Write an answer to Question 3.

At the end of every chapter in the *Reading Study Guide,* you will find a Glossary and a section called After You Read. The Glossary gives definitions of important words used in the chapter. After You Read is a two-page chapter review. Use After You Read to identify those parts of the chapter that you need to study more for the test on the chapter.

Strategy: Review all of the of Terms & Names before completing Parts A and B of After You Read.

Try This: Use the *Reading Study Guide* for Chapter 1 to answer Questions A 1–5.

Name   Period   Date

Chapter 2 The Expansion and Fall of Rome

Glossary/After You Read

adviser someone who gives or offers advice

arena an enclosed area where shows or sports events are given

authority a source of expert information

bold brave; showing no fear

capital a city where a state or national government is located

contain to hold back; restrain

establish begin or set up; create

key very important

merchant a person who buys or sells goods

realistic very much like real life or nature

series a number of similar people or things in a row or following one another

structure something made up of a number

Terms & Names

A. If the statement is true, write "true" on underlined word or words to make it tr

_____ **1.** A republic is a gr powerful ruler.

_____ **2.** The Byzantine Er

_____ **3.** The schism of 10 creation of the R Church in the Eas

_____ **4.** One of the main Eastern Orthodox

_____ **5.** Roman builders cities and towns.

B. Write the letter of the name or term tha

_____ **6.** Roman emperor who moved the Rome to Byzantium

_____ **7.** Leader of the Franks who conqu a Frankish kingdom

_____ **8.** Powerful ruler of the Byzantine

_____ **9.** The philosophy developed by G

_____ **10.** First leader of the Roman Empi

CHAPTER 2

Strategy: Review the chapter summaries before completing the Main Ideas questions. Write a complete sentence for every answer.

Try This: In your own words, what is Question 11 asking for?

Name   Period

Main Ideas

11. How was the government of the Roman republic different from the government of the Roman Empire?

_____

_____

12. What internal problems weakened the Roman Empire and led to its fall?

_____

_____

13. What changes did Constantine make to the Roman Empire?

_____

_____

14. What helped Constantinople become a center for business and trade?

_____

_____

15. What caused the split in Christianity during the Byzantine Empire?

_____

_____

_____

16. What legal principles did Roman law promote?

_____

_____

Thinking Critically

17. Making Inferences What role did Rome's internal problems play in its conquest by foreign invaders?

_____

_____

18. Comparing and Contrasting In what ways were Augustus and Justinian alike?

_____

_____

Strategy: Write one or two paragraphs for every Thinking Critically question.

Try This: In your own words, what is Question 17 asking for?

Lesson 1 Geography of the World

BEFORE YOU READ

In this lesson, you will learn about the many elements that make up geography.

AS YOU READ

Use this diagram to list the main ideas about the geography of the world. Answering the question at the end of each section will help you fill in the diagram.

TERMS & NAMES

- **geography** the study of Earth's features
- **continent** a large landmass
- **landform** a feature of the earth's surface
- **weather** the condition of the atmosphere at a particular place and time
- **climate** the typical weather conditions at a particular location over a period of time

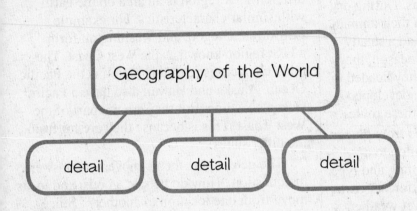

Looking at Earth

(pages 9–10)

What covers the surface of the Earth?

Geography is the study of the earth's features, such as rivers and deserts. Geographers are people who study geography. Geographers also study how living things and Earth's features interact. Geography has shaped where people lived and how people lived. It has also influenced historical decisions.

Geographers divide the world into seven **continents.** The seven continents are Africa, Antarctica, Asia, Australia, Europe, North America, and South America. All continents are large landmasses, but their sizes vary greatly. That is because geographers define continents not just by size. They also consider landforms and common cultural characteristics.

The earth has many types of **landforms.** They include mountains, plateaus, hills, valleys, and plains. Landforms have had a strong influence on the way people live. For example, farming in a mountainous region is different from farming in a plains region.

Nearly 75 percent of the earth is covered by water. Some of the water is fresh and some is salt water. Only fresh water is drinkable. Bodies of water include oceans, lakes, and rivers. Since ancient times, people used waterways to transport goods. Water travel helped people to communicate with each other. People have also harvested fish from oceans, lakes, and rivers.

1. How has geography shaped the lives of people?

_____

_____

_____

_____

CHAPTER 1

Climate, Weather, and Vegetation

(pages 10–11)

What is the difference between climate and weather?

The condition of the atmosphere at a particular place and time is called **weather. Climate** is the typical weather conditions at a particular location over a period of time.

Throughout history, climate has affected the way people lived. For example, the Arabian Peninsula has a very hot, dry climate. This region also has short rainy seasons. During dry seasons, people would move with their animal herds. They went to a place that had a steady source of water. During the rainy season, they would move again. At this time, they headed to pastures. Over time, many people developed a way of life around moving along these routes.

Vegetation, or plant life, varies from place to place. The types of plants common to a place depend on temperature, rainfall, and type of soil. For example, tropical rain forests grow in areas that always have warm, wet weather.

Vegetation also affects ways of life. For example, a thousand years ago Europe had many forests. People used these forests for fuel, hunting, and building materials. In contrast, parts of Southwest Asia have very few trees. People there got what they needed through trade.

2. What factors determine which types of plants are common to a place?

_____

_____

Five Themes of Geography

(pages 12–13)

How do geographers organize the study of geography?

The geographic theme location answers the question "Where is it?" Absolute location is the exact place where a geographic feature is found. Relative location describes where a geographic feature is found in comparison to

places around it. For example, California is south of Oregon.

The geographic theme place answers the question "What is it like there?" Place deals with the physical features of a location. It also deals with features made by people. These are called human features. A natural harbor is an example of a physical feature. A skyscraper is an example of a human feature.

The geographic theme region answers the question "How are places similar and different?" A region is an area on the earth with similar characteristics. For example, California, Oregon, and Washington form a U.S. region known as the West Coast. The main characteristic of this region is the Pacific Ocean. Alaska and Hawaii also have a Pacific Ocean coastline. But they are not part of the West Coast. This is because they are far from the other states.

The geographic theme movement answers the question "How do people, goods, and ideas move from one location to another?" Since ancient times, peoples, goods, and ideas have moved from place to place.

The geographic theme human-environment interaction answers the question "How do people relate to the physical world?" Throughout history, people have used what the environment offers. By doing this, they have changed the way they lived. Historians study what people did in the past. One basic influence on what people did was the conditions in which they lived—their geography. Understanding geography is an important part of being a historian.

3. What are the five themes of geography?

_____

_____

_____

_____

_____

Lesson 2 Mapping the World

CHAPTER 1

BEFORE YOU READ

In this lesson, you will learn about the history of mapmaking. You will also learn how to read maps and how technology is used to make maps.

AS YOU READ

Use this chart to take notes about the history of mapmaking, reading maps, and making maps. Answering the question at the end of each section will help you fill in the chart.

Section	Summary
History of Mapmaking	
Features of Maps	
Technology Changes Mapmaking	

TERMS & NAMES

- **cartography** the skills and methods used to make maps
- **projection** a way of drawing a flat map that helps to reduce distortion
- **hemisphere** one half of the earth
- **latitude** imaginary lines that run the same way as the equator
- **longitude** imaginary lines that go around the earth over the north and south poles

History of Mapmaking

(pages 15–16)

What were important advances in maps?

Maps can help us understand how ancient people saw their world. They can also show us where historical events happened. In addition, maps can show us how historical events happened. The skills and methods people use to make maps are called **cartography.** The oldest map we have today was made on a clay tablet in Babylon. It is more than 4,000 years old.

Ptolemy was an ancient Greek geographer. He wrote works about making more accurate maps. Over the years, the works of Ptolemy became lost to Europeans. In the 800s, Muslim scholars translated the works of Ptolemy into Arabic. His ideas influenced many Arab mapmakers.

Around 1155, the first known printed map appeared. It was part of a Chinese encyclopedia. The technology of printing allowed more copies of a map to be made.

Europeans rediscovered the works of Ptolemy in the 1400s. These works helped European cartographers make more accurate maps. At the time, most mapmakers knew that the earth was round. But this information presented them with a problem. A flat map of the round earth will show some parts of the earth as smaller than they really are. In addition, it will show other parts of the earth as larger than they really are. This stretching or shrinking is called distortion. To deal with this problem, mapmakers developed a method called **projection.** A projection is a way of drawing a flat map that helps reduce distortion.

Better maps helped European sailors.

1. Why did mapmakers develop a method called projection?

_____

_____

READING STUDY GUIDE CONTINUED

Features of Maps

(pages 17–19)

What are the main elements of maps?

On maps, Earth can be divided into two equal halves. Each half is called a **hemisphere.** An imaginary line is used to divide Earth into north and south halves. This line is called the equator. The half of Earth north of the equator is the Northern Hemisphere. The half south of the equator is the Southern Hemisphere.

Earth also has an imaginary line that divides it into east and west halves. This line is called the prime meridian. The half west of the prime meridian is the Western Hemisphere. The half east of the prime meridian is the Eastern Hemisphere.

Imaginary lines that run the same way as the equator are called **latitude** lines. They are used to locate places in the north and south hemispheres. **Longitude** lines are imaginary lines that go around Earth over the north and south poles. They are used to locate places in the east and west hemispheres.

How do you find the absolute location of a place? By using a grid of latitude and longitude lines. The absolute location of a place is the point where the latitude and longitude lines cross.

Physical maps show the type of landforms and bodies of water found in an area. They also show the shape of a region. Political divisions, like countries, are not the focus of physical maps.

Political maps show features on Earth's surface that people created. A political map might include cities and countries.

Thematic maps focus on specific types of information. These maps can show climate, natural resources, historical trends, and population.

2. How do you find absolute location? Explain.

_____

_____

_____

Technology Changes Mapmaking

(pages 19–21)

How can new technology make better maps?

The GPS or Global Positioning System can let a person know his or her exact location on earth. GPS uses a series of 24 satellites. These satellites are called Navstars. Each Navstar sends radio signals to earth. People can pick up these signals by using a certain type of receiver. The receivers display latitude, longitude, altitude, and time. Now, hikers, sailors, drivers, and of course mapmakers use GPS to figure out there location.

Geostationary Operational Environment Satellite (GOES) is a weather satellite. This satellite flies in orbit at the same speed as the earth's rotation. As a result, it always views the same area. GOES gathers information that helps people to forecast the weather.

The Geographic Information System (GIS) stores information about the world in a computer. GIS is able to combine information from many sources. It can then show this information in the form of a map.

Geographers often use GIS to solve problems. First geographers must decide what kind of information will help solve a problem. They then divide this information into layers and enter it into the GIS. Geographers can study the information more quickly, and in more detail.

Historians can use GIS to make layered historical maps. They accomplish this by entering historical data into the GIS.

3. How does GIS create a map?

_____

_____

_____

_____

_____

_____

Lesson 3 Discovering the Past

BEFORE YOU READ

In this lesson, you will learn about the work of archaeologists and anthropologists. You will also learn how archaeology affects history.

AS YOU READ

Use this diagram to take notes about what archaeologists do. Then, write a general statement about the work of archaeologists. Answering the questions at the end of each section will help you fill in the diagram.

TERMS & NAMES
• **archaeology** the recovery and study of physical evidence from the past
• **artifact** an object made by a human
• **excavation** digging to find buried evidence
• **anthropology** the study of humans and human cultures
• **culture** a way of life shared by a group of people

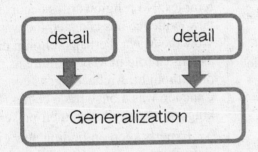

detail   detail

Generalization

Digging Up the Past

(pages 25–26)

How do we learn about ancient societies?

Archaeology focuses on finding and studying physical evidence about the past. These scientists are called archaeologists. They search for **artifacts** from a time period. Tools, pottery, and jewelry are examples of artifacts.

Archaeologists also look for other evidence of past human activity. For example, the remains of a house might provide clues about how people lived.

How do archaeologists find these clues? First of all, they must find a location, or site. Next they survey the site. This involves making a map of the area. Then they collect any artifacts that lie on the surface. The place where each artifact was found is noted on the map.

Archaeologists then dig to find buried evidence. This type of digging is called **excavation.** After finding objects,

archaeologists record them. They describe, photograph, and count the evidence.

Finally, archaeologists try to draw conclusions from evidence. To do this, they ask questions. For example, an archaeologist might ask, "How was this pottery made?" Archaeologists then test their conclusions against new evidence that they find. Sometimes the new evidence does not support their conclusions. If this happens, archaeologists start the process over.

1. How do archaeologists record evidence?

_____

_____

_____

_____

_____

READING STUDY GUIDE CONTINUED

Studying Humans

(pages 26–27)

What do anthropologists study?

Anthropology is the study of humans and human cultures. Physical anthropologists study the physical characteristics of humans. These humans may live now or may have lived in the past.

Cultural anthropologists study human culture. **Culture** includes the arts, beliefs, customs, language, and technology of a people. These anthropologists study artifacts as well as the beliefs and values of a culture. Like archaeologists, anthropologists ask questions based on what they want to find out. They also test their conclusions against new evidence.

2. What types of work do anthropologists do?

_____

_____

_____

Changing Views of the Past

(pages 27–28)

Why do theories about the past change?

The Maya developed a civilization between A.D. 250 and 900. It was located in what is today Central America. The Maya created huge temples and palaces.

Cancuén was a busy Maya city. Archaeologists found Cancuén in 1905. At the time, they thought it was just a small Maya city. Then, in 2000, archaeologists discovered a huge palace. Houses and workshops surrounded the palace.

The Maya cities found before Cancuén always seemed to have temples. Because of this, many archaeologists and anthropologists believed that Maya cities had mostly a religious purpose. Scientists thought that Maya kings based their power on religion and warfare.

But Cancuén is a Maya city with no temples. No religious rites occurred there. This new evidence has changed the way scholars view the Maya. Perhaps religion did not play as large a role in Maya culture as people once thought. Archaeologists concluded that Cancuén was a busy trade center. The Maya kings at this city based their power on trade.

Experts keep on finding new evidence about Mayan cities. As a result, they continue to debate the role of religion in Mayan culture. As we have seen, new evidence strongly effects the way people view history. It can cause archaeologists and anthropologists to change their views about the past.

3. What did archaeologists discover after excavating Cancuén?

_____

_____

_____

Lesson 4 Interpreting the Past

BEFORE YOU READ

In this lesson, you will learn how historians study and interpret the past.

AS YOU READ

Use this diagram to take notes about how historians study and learn about the past. Answering the question at the end of each section will help you fill in the diagram.

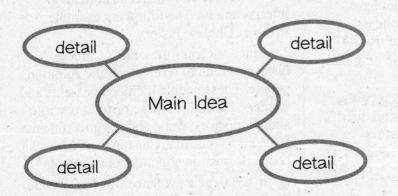

TERMS & NAMES
• **history** the study of past events
• **historian** a person who studies and writes about the past
• **primary source** a document or artifact created during the period being studied
• **oral history** stories, customs, and songs that a culture has told and passed from generation to generation
• **secondary source** a work written about a historical event by someone who was not actually there

The Story of the Past

(pages 31–32)

Why do historians ask questions about the past?

History is the study of past events. A **historian** is a person who studies and writes about the past.

History helps us learn about today and our future. Historians often study a single event and who was involved in that event. They are also concerned about why the event happened the way it did. In addition, they look into how the event affected what happened next. To find this information, historians ask questions. Below is a list of some historical questions. Try to apply them to a history you are familiar with, maybe your own history.

- In what order did events happen?
- How have belief systems developed and changed?
- How have societies dealt with differences among their people?

- How are societies similar and different?
- Why did things happen the way they did?
- How have groups or societies related to each other and what have been the results?

1. Why do people study history?

_____

_____

How Historians Work

(pages 32–33)

How do historians answer their questions?

How do historians find answers to their questions? Like detectives, historians study evidence. Then they explain the meaning of the evidence.

A **primary source** is a document or artifact created during the historical period being studied. Written primary sources can include military records, diaries, and private

CHAPTER 1

letters. Not all primary sources are written. Artifacts can also be primary sources. Pottery and tools are examples of artifacts that can be primary sources. A primary source helps a historian answer his or her questions.

A **secondary source** is a work written about a historical event by someone who was not there. Historians study and learn from secondary sources. Newspapers, books, and paintings are possible secondary sources. Secondary sources often have insights about historical events. Many times, primary sources about the same event do not have these insights. For example, a secondary source about Columbus might note that he had not sailed to Asia. That is something that Columbus himself never realized.

Societies often have no written records. When this happens, historians rely on their oral history as a resource. **Oral history** includes the stories, customs, and songs that a culture has told. This type of history is passed from generation to generation.

Historians carefully examine evidence. This examination helps historians learn more about a document's point of view. The examination involves asking a series of questions.

- Why was the document written or recorded?
- Who was the document written for?
- Was the document intended to be private (a diary), personal (a letter), or public (an official document)?
- What was the author's purpose in writing the document?
- How might the author's background have influenced his or her writing?

The answers to these questions can tell a historian if the document is useful. For example, say you are researching the history of factories. You find a secondary source claiming that factories help people. A factory owner wrote the source. This person might have written the article to convince people to accept

his point of view. A historian must consider this possibility.

2. What do historians use evidence for?

_____

_____

Interpreting History

(pages 34–35)

What do historians do with all their evidence?
New evidence can change historical interpretations. The following example involves Chinese history.

Since ancient times, most Chinese historians did not write about the common people. These people included peasants and farmers. Instead, Chinese historians wrote about emperors, wars, and the government. Because of this, many histories of China have little information about common people.

In 1900, new evidence was found about the lives of common people in China. A sealed cave was discovered in Dunhuang, China. It contained documents created between A.D. 400 and A.D. 1000. The cave included adoption forms and local histories. Scholars also found books for students and calendars.

These records are primary sources. By studying them, historians have gained a better understanding of how Chinese farmers lived. They learned that farmers received land from the government. They also learned that farmers often organized themselves. Historians now have new views of Chinese history.

3. How can new evidence change historical interpretation?

_____

_____

_____

Chapter 1 The Tools of History

Glossary/After You Read

shaped influenced; affected

slopes stretches of round that slant upward or downward

atmosphere the gas that surrounds a body in space; especially the air that surrounds the earth

methods regular ways of doing something

imaginary not real; existing only in the imagination

accurate free from mistakes; exactly right

buried in the ground and covered with earth

evidence objects, facts, or signs that help one come to a conclusion

period a length or portion of time

sealed closed or shut

Terms & Names

A. Circle the name or term that best completes each sentence.

1. The condition of the atmosphere at a particular place and time is called _____.

   climate   weather   season

2. Imaginary lines that go around the earth over the north and south poles are called _____ lines.

   longitude   latitude   circumference

3. Scientists who focus on finding and studying physical evidence are called _____.

   historians   anthropologists   archaeologists

4. The study of past events is called _____.

   cartography   geography   history

5. A series of 24 satellites that can let a person know his or her exact location on earth is called _____.

   GPS   GOES   GIS

B. Write a letter of the term that matches the description.

_____ **6.** one half of the earth

_____ **7.** a way of life shared by a group of people

_____ **8.** stories, customs, and songs passed from generation to generation

_____ **9.** a feature of the earth's surface

_____ **10.** a way of drawing a flat map that helps reduce distortion

_____ **11.** an object made by a human

a. landform

b. artifact

c. projection

d. oral history

e. hemisphere

f. culture

READING STUDY GUIDE CONTINUED

Main Ideas

12. What geographic theme answers the question "How do people relate to the physical world?" Give an example of this theme.

_____

_____

13. What type of satellite is the Geostationary Operational Environment Satellite (GOES)? How does it work?

_____

_____

14. What procedure do archaeologists follow at a site before they excavate?

_____

_____

15. How did the discovery in the Dunhuang cave help historians?

_____

_____

16. Why does archaeological evidence often fail to provide a complete picture about a culture?

_____

_____

Thinking Critically

17. Forming and Supporting Opinions Do you think Mayan kings based their power more on religion and warfare or on trade?

_____

_____

_____

18. Making Inferences Why do you think primary sources often lack insight into the event being described?

_____

_____

Lesson 1 The Rise and Expansion of Rome

BEFORE YOU READ

In this section, you will read how Rome grew from a small village to a great empire.

AS YOU READ

As you read about the rise and expansion of Rome, use this chart to record major events on a time line like the one shown below.

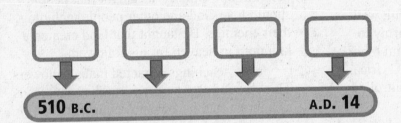

510 B.C.   A.D. **14**

CHAPTER 2

The Origins of Rome

(pages 47–48)

How did Rome begin?

From about 700 to 500 B.C., three different groups lived on the Italian peninsula. They were the Latins, Greeks, and Etruscans. The Latins built the original settlement of Rome. They are considered the first Romans.

Rome's climate and location helped it grow. The region enjoyed cool, rainy winters that were good for farming. Rome's location near the Apennines mountain range protected it from harsh weather and foreign invaders. Rome's location near the Tiber River helped the Romans build a trade network throughout Italy and along the Mediterranean Sea.

During the eighth century B.C., Rome became a kingdom. It remained a kingdom until 510 B.C., when the Romans rebelled against a harsh ruler named Tarquin. They forced Tarquin to flee the kingdom. After that, the Romans refused to be ruled by kings. They instead decided to create a government based on the will of the people.

1. Why did the kingdom of Rome end?

_____

_____

_____

_____

From Republic to Empire

(pages 48–49)

Why did Rome change from a republic to an empire?

After removing Tarquin, the Romans established a **republic.** This is a form of government in which powers rests with citizens, who vote to select their leaders. Rome remained a republic for the next 500 years. In the Roman Republic all free-born males could vote. Women had few rights.

The Romans created a powerful, well-organized army. They used their army to conquer all of modern-day Italy and other lands including Carthage in North Africa. Through conquest the Romans controlled much of the Mediterranean Sea.

As the Roman Republic expanded, it became harder for Rome's rulers to keep order. Conflict between different groups within the country led to a civil war. In 45 B.C. Roman general Julius Caesar ended the war and brought order to Rome. He then named himself sole ruler. This ended the Roman Republic. A year later Caesar's enemies killed him.

Rome's leaders competed for power. Caesar's adopted son Octavian won the power struggle and became Rome's ruler. He took the title **Augustus,** or "divine one." Under Augustus, Rome became an **empire.** An empire is a group of different people or territories led by an all-powerful ruler. The ruler of an empire is known as the **emperor.** The rule of Augustus began a time of peace, prosperity, and growth for Rome.

Augustus died in A.D. 14. After his death, the policies he began helped Rome continue to expand and gain power. By the second century A.D. the Roman Empire reached is largest size. It included between about 60 and 100 million people of many different cultures and religions.

2. What helped Rome become a large empire?

_____

_____

The Rise of Christianity

(pages 50–51)

How did Christianity grow so powerful?

During the Roman Empire the religion known as **Christianity** developed. It became one of the world's major religions. Christianity is based on the teachings of Jesus. Jesus was born in the Roman province of Judea. Jesus was a Jew. Many of his teachings contained ideas from his Jewish faith, especially the belief in one God. Jesus taught that people should love God and other people including their enemies. He taught that God created a kingdom in heaven for his followers.

Jesus' teachings attracted many followers. This worried Roman leaders. They saw Jesus as a threat to their own power. Eventually, officials arrested Jesus and put him to death.

After his death, the followers of Jesus spread his teachings throughout the Roman Empire. Early Christians risked their lives for their new faith. Many refused to worship Roman gods because they believed in only one God. As a result, Roman officials jailed and killed many Christians. Despite this, the new religion continued to spread.

3. Why did Roman leaders treat Christians harshly?

_____

_____

_____

Lesson 2 Decline and Fall of the Empire

BEFORE YOU READ

In the last section, you read about the expansion of Roman power and the growth of Christianity. In this lesson you will learn about the causes of the decline and fall of the Roman Empire.

AS YOU READ

Use a graphic organizer like the one below to list the factors that weakened the Roman Empire.

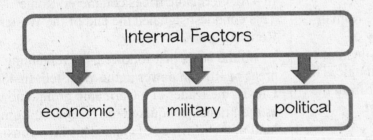

TERMS & NAMES

- **Constantine** Roman emperor who declared an end to all attacks on Christians and allowed them to worship freely
- **Clovis** leader of a Germanic group known as the Franks, who conquered Roman land in Gaul

Internal Weaknesses Threaten Rome

(pages 53–54)

What internal problems weakened the Roman Empire?

Late in the second century, Rome stopped expanding and adding new lands. Without new conquests, the empire had no new sources of wealth. In time, the government faced serious economic problems. It lacked the money to pay for the army and other expenses of running a large empire. As a result, Roman officials had to raise taxes. This made life harder for many citizens.

Other aspects of Roman society suffered as well. Higher education became too costly for many Romans. In addition, distributing news across the large empire became harder. As a result, people grew less informed about government and public affairs.

Agriculture also declined. Constant war and overuse of farmland ruined farmland. Harvests yielded fewer crops. The use of slavery added to the problem. The Romans used many slaves as farm workers. This kept the Romans from making improvements in technology that might have led to better harvests. As Roman agriculture grew worse, diseases and hunger spread and the population declined.

The Roman Empire also faced military and political problems. Roman soldiers became less willing to follow orders and less loyal to the government. Average citizens also became less loyal and less involved in public life. In earlier times Roman citizens were active in government and public affairs. In time, Roman leaders became more interested in getting rich than in public service. As a result, many citizens lost their pride and trust in government. All of these problems weakened the empire.

1. What problems weakened the empire?

_____

_____

_____

READING STUDY GUIDE CONTINUED

Rome Divides into East and West

(pages 54–55)

What changes did Rome undergo?

Despite Rome's many problems, two strong emperors kept the empire going for another 200 years. The emperor Diocletian divided Rome into eastern and western parts. This made the empire easier to govern. **Constantine** succeeded Diocletian as emperor. He made two decisions that changed the empire. First, in A.D. 313, he ended attacks on Christians. By allowing Christians to workshop freely, he helped Christianity grow. In A.D. 330, Constantine moved the capital of the Roman Empire from Rome to the Greek city of Byzantium farther to the east. After the move, the city became known as Constantinople. The new capital signaled a shift in power from the western part of the empire to the east.

2. What changes did Constantine make to the Roman Empire?

_____

_____

_____

Fall of the Roman Empire

(pages 55–56)

How did Rome fall?

Rome faced many internal problems. The empire also faced threats from foreign invaders. During the late 300s, many Germanic peoples living outside Rome's borders invaded Roman lands. Most of the invasion occurred in the Western Roman Empire. The invading groups came for many reasons. Some wanted better land or wealth. Others were fleeing a group of Asian invaders known as the Huns. In 476, Germanic tribes conquered Rome This conquest signaled the end of the Western Roman Empire.

In the years that followed, the remaining areas of Roman power in the West fell. In 486, **Clovis,** the leader of a Germanic group known as the Franks, conquered the rest of the Roman land in the province of Gaul. This area consists of present-day France and Switzerland. Clovis founded a Frankish kingdom that grew large and powerful.

While the western half of the Roman Empire fell, the eastern half survived for another thousand years. It became known as the Byzantine Empire.

3. What key event took place in 476?

_____

_____

_____

Lesson 3 The Early Byzantine Empire

BEFORE YOU READ

In the last section, you read how the Roman Empire split into east and West. The western part fell to invaders. In this lesson you will learn how the eastern half became the Byzantine Empire.

AS YOU READ

As you read Lesson 3, use a chart like the one below to list the main causes and effects of the split in Christianity.

Causes	Effects

TERMS & NAMES

- **Byzantine Empire** the eastern half of the former Roman Empire
- **Justinian I** powerful ruler of the Byzantine Empire
- **Justinian Code** a legal code that organized much of Byzantine life
- **schism** an official split of Christianity that led to two new Christian churches
- **Roman Catholic** Christian church in the West
- **Orthodox** Christian church in the East

Justinian Builds a New Rome

(pages 59–60)

What were the main characteristics of the Byzantine Empire?

In 476, the Western Roman Empire fell. The eastern half of the empire survived and became known as the **Byzantine Empire.** The empire soon became strong and powerful. This was due in large part to the efforts of one the empire's early rulers **Justinian I.**

Justinian ruled from 527 to 565. He expanded the empire and recaptured some of the land Roman rulers had lost. He also developed a law code known as the **Justinian Code.** The code regulated much of Byzantine life and served the empire for 900 years. Justinian also undertook many large public works and building projects including the rebuilding of a famous church, the Hagia Sophia. Justinian was aided in his efforts by his wife and trusted advisor, Theodora.

1. What were some of Justinian's main achievements?

_____

_____

_____

_____

The Rise of Constantinople

(page 60)

What was life like in Constantinople?

Constantinople was the capital of the Byzantine Empire. Its location between Europe and southwest helped it to become a center of business and trade.

Merchant stalls lined the street and sold products from distant corners of Asia, Africa, and Europe. The citizens of Constantinople could enjoy many attractions, including numerous activities at the city's large arena, the Hippodrome.

2. How did Constantinople's location affect its growth?

_____

_____

_____

_____

Disagreements Split Christianity

(pages 61–63)

What two churches emerged from the split in Christianity?

Because of its location between Europe and Asia, ideas from both areas influenced the Byzantine Empire. The Byzantine Empire developed a unique culture. For example, Christianity developed differently in the Byzantine Empire than it did in the West.

In the West, Christianity had a well-organized structure with priests, bishops, and the pope as the leader of the entire Christian Church.

As the Byzantine Empire grew, popes and Byzantine emperors often disagreed. Both felt they should have the final say in religious matters. The two sides became involved in a major conflict over the use of icons. These are religious images that many Eastern Christians used to aid their prayers. In 730, the Byzantine Emperor Leo III banned the use of icons. He viewed them as idol worship, or the belief in false gods. The pope favored the use of icons. He excommunicated, or removed from the church, the Byzantine emperor.

Further conflicts between Christian leaders in the East and West led to a **schism,** or official split, in 1054. This split resulted in the creation of two new churches: the **Roman Catholic** Church in the West and the **Orthodox** Church in the East.

The two churches were alike in some ways, but were organized differently. Each also followed beliefs that set them apart. For example, each group viewed relations between the church and the state differently. In the Roman Catholic Church, the pope claimed authority over kings and emperors as well as the church. In the Eastern Orthodox Church, the emperor ruled over the patriarch, the religious leader of the Orthodox Church.

3. How did the schism of 1054 affect Christianity?

_____

_____

_____

_____

Lesson 4 The Legacy of Rome

BEFORE YOU READ

In this last section, you will read about the achievements of the Romans in the arts, law, engineering, and government.

AS YOU READ

As you read Lesson 4, create a graphic organizer like the one below to show the lasting achievements of the Roman Empire.

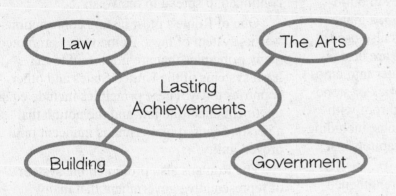

TERMS & NAMES

- **mosaic** a picture made out of many small colored tiles or pieces of glass
- **Stoicism** philosophy that stresses the importance of virtue, duty, and endurance in life
- **aqueduct** bridge-like structures that brought fresh water to Roman towns

CHAPTER 2

The Impact of Roman Culture

(pages 67–68)

How did Roman culture influence later societies?

The Romans borrowed from the Greeks to develop aspects of their culture. Roman artists, thinkers, and writers combined Greek ideas and arts with their own ideas to create Roman styles. These styles influenced many later societies. Roman artists popularized a type of art called mosaic. A **mosaic** is a picture made out of many small colored tiles or pieces of glass. Roman artists also became skilled at sculpture. They adopted the realistic style of sculpture created by the Greeks.

The Romans also borrowed much of their philosophy from the Greeks. Many Romans followed the philosophy of **Stoicism,** which was developed by the Greek thinker Zeno. Stoicism stressed the importance of duty and helping each other and society. It asked people to take an active role in public affairs. The beliefs of stoicism helped build a strong sense of citizenship among Romans.

As the Romans conquered Europe, the Roman language of Latin spread. Latin influenced many languages spoken today. Spanish, Italian, French, Portuguese, and Romanian are based on Latin. In addition, more than half of all English words are based on Latin.

1. What were three ways Roman culture influenced later societies?

_____

_____

_____

_____

Architectural and Engineering Feats

(page 69)

What advances did the Romans make in engineering?

Roman engineers made many advances in architecture and building. Roman builders used arches, vaults, and domes to create higher and larger buildings than ever before. An arch is a curved opening that holds up a building. The Romans used arches to build large buildings like the Colosseum, a giant outdoor stadium. Roman builders also used arches to build **aqueducts.** These are bridge-like structures that bring fresh water into cities and towns. A vault is an arched brick or stone ceiling or roof. A dome is a round roof with many sides. Many modern buildings, including the U.S. Capitol and many state capitols, use arches, domes, and vaults.

The Romans protected and strengthened their empire by improving transportation. They built some 50,000 miles of roads. Many of these roads were built to help the Roman army move more quickly and easily. Many modern highways in Europe follow routes first laid out by the Romans.

2. What three building styles did the Romans use most often?

   _____

   _____

   _____

Contributions to Religion and Law

(pages 70–71)

How did the Romans contribute to religion and law?

The Romans contributed to religion by supporting Christianity and helping it grow. Roman rulers eventually made Christianity the official religion of the empire. After the Western Roman Empire fell, Christianity continued to spread in the West.

One of Rome's most lasting contributions was its system of laws. Roman laws promoted many principles that are important to the legal systems of the United States and other countries today. These principles include equal treatment under the law and the notion that a person accused of a crime is innocent until proven guilty.

The Romans also promoted the system of representative government that many nations use today. When Rome was a republic, it created various assemblies, including a senate, to make laws and represent the views of the people. In the United States today, the House of Representatives and the Senate act as representative assemblies for the people. Many other nations have similar forms of representative government.

3. What contributions did the Romans make to the area of law?

   _____

   _____

   _____

   _____

Chapter 2 The Expansion and Fall of Rome

Glossary/After You Read

adviser someone who gives or offers advice

arena an enclosed area where shows or sports events are given

authority a source of expert information

bold brave; showing no fear

capital a city where a state or national government is located

contain to hold back; restrain

establish begin or set up; create

key very important

merchant a person who buys or sells goods

realistic very much like real life or nature

series a number of similar people or things in a row or following one another

structure something made up of a number of parts

Terms & Names

A. If the statement is true, write "true" on the line. If it is false, change the underlined word or words to make it true.

_____ **1.** A <u>republic</u> is a group of different people or territories led by a single all-powerful ruler.

_____ **2.** The <u>Byzantine Empire</u> was the eastern half of the former Roman Empire.

_____ **3.** The <u>schism</u> of 1054 was a split within Christian Church that led to the creation of the Roman Catholic Church in the West and the Orthodox Church in the East.

_____ **4.** One of the main differences between the <u>Roman Catholic</u> Church and Eastern <u>Orthodoxy</u> was over the relations between the church and state.

_____ **5.** Roman builders became skilled at building <u>mosaics</u> to provide water for cities and towns.

B. Write the letter of the name or term that matches the description.

_____ **6.** Roman emperor who moved the capital of the empire from Rome to Byzantium

_____ **7.** Leader of the Franks who conquered Roman lands and founded a Frankish kingdom

_____ **8.** Powerful ruler of the Byzantine Empire who created a law code

_____ **9.** The philosophy developed by Greek thinker Zeno

_____ **10.** First leader of the Roman Empire, known as the "divine one"

a. Constantine

b. Stoicism

c. Justinian

d. Augustus

e. Clovis

READING STUDY GUIDE CONTINUED

Main Ideas

11. How was the government of the Roman republic different from the government of the Roman Empire?

_____

_____

12. What internal problems weakened the Roman Empire and led to its fall?

_____

_____

13. What changes did Constantine make to the Roman Empire?

_____

_____

14. What helped Constantinople become a center for business and trade?

_____

_____

15. What caused the split in Christianity during the Byzantine Empire?

_____

_____

16. What legal principles did Roman law promote?

_____

_____

Thinking Critically

17. Making Inferences What role did Rome's internal problems play in its conquest by foreign invaders?

_____

_____

18. Comparing and Contrasting In what ways were Augustus and Justinian alike?

_____

_____

Lesson 1 Life on the Arabian Peninsula

BEFORE YOU READ

In this lesson, you will learn about how the Arabian Peninsula influenced the way of life of the Arab people.

AS YOU READ

Use this cluster diagram to take notes about life on the Arabian Peninsula. Answering the question at the end of each section will help you fill in the chart.

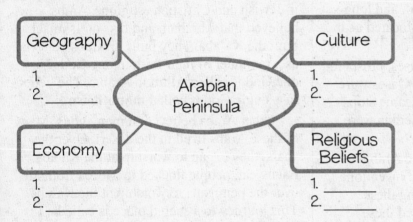

TERMS & NAMES
• **nomad** people who move from place to place instead of settling permanently
• **oasis** a desert area that contains water
• **clan** families of people related by blood or marriage
• **Allah** in Islam, the name of God
• **monotheism** belief in a single God
• **pilgrimage** a journey to a sacred place

A Desert Culture

(pages 85–86)

How did the geography of the Arabian peninsula encourage a nomadic way of life?

The deserts of the Arabian Peninsula cover hundreds of thousands of square miles. One of the largest of these deserts is called the Rub al Khali. Rub al Khali is an Arabic word. It means "the empty quarter."

The Arabian Peninsula is a region of southwest Asia. It lies between the Red Sea and the Persian Gulf. It is about one-fourth the size of the United States. The region is very dry. Only a small amount of land receives enough water to support farming.

Arab herders called Bedouins have lived on this land for centuries. Bedouins are **nomads.** They move from place to place to find water and grazing land for their herds. This movement happens within a fixed area. The path that Bedouins follow is affected by the type of landscape they must cross, the amount of rainfall, and the location of the **oasis,** a desert area that contains water.

Bedouins interacted with people who lived at oases. These people did not move from place to place. Instead, they remain settled at their oasis. These settled people gave Bedouins food and clothes. In return, the Bedouins protected them from other Bedouins.

Bedouins organized themselves into groups called **clans.** Clans provided security in the harsh desert. Bedouins were proud of their fighting skills. The fighting skills of the Bedouin also helped them to serve the Islamic Empire. They became the core of the army that helped form this empire.

1. Why does the Arabian peninsula have small amounts of farming?

_____

_____

READING STUDY GUIDE CONTINUED

Crossroads of Three Continents

(pages 87–88)

What made the Arabian peninsula important for trade?

The Arabian Peninsula is in a good location for trade. It is a crossroads of three continents—Asia, Africa, and Europe. Also, bodies of water surround it.

Many Arabs had moved to market towns or oases by the early 600s. Market towns grew into cities because of trade. Larger cities became centers for local, regional, and long-distance trade. These cities were located near the western coast of Arabia.

Other areas, such as larger oases, prospered because they supported farming. Oases were also important for trade. They became stops along trade routes. Mecca and Medina were such oasis cities.

Sea and land routes connected Arabia to major trade centers. Products and inventions from three continents moved along these routes. Camel caravans transported these goods. Merchants traded animals, textiles, paper, steel, and crops.

Trade was also important in cultural exchange. Merchants carried information, as well as products. For example, trade helped to spread Judaism and Christianity.

2. Why is the Arabian Peninsula in a good location for trade?

_____

_____

_____

The Holy City of Mecca

(pages 88–89)

Why was Mecca important as a religious center?

Mecca was important as a trading center. But it was important as a religious center as well. Caravans stopped in Mecca during certain holy months. They brought people who came to worship at a religious shrine called the Ka'aba.

Arabs connected the Ka'aba with a Biblical figure named Abraham. Abraham is important in Jewish and Christian religions. Arabs believed that Abraham and his son Ishmael built the Ka'aba. They built it, Arabs believed, as a reminder of their faith in one God. This one God is called **Allah** in Arabic. The belief in a single God is called **monotheism.**

Other Arabs believed in many gods. Many of these Arabs lived in the desert. Over the years, they began to worship at the Ka'aba. Each year, people flocked to Mecca from all over the peninsula to worship at the Ka'aba. This journey to a sacred place is called a **pilgrimage.**

Many Jews and Christians lived in Arab lands. Some Arabs blended Christian and Jewish beliefs with their own traditions. It was into this environment of religious diversity that Muhammad was born. He was born in Mecca in A.D. 570. Muhammad became the prophet of the Islamic religion.

3. What religious traditions were practiced on the Arabian Peninsula before 570?

_____

_____

CHAPTER 3

Lesson 2 Islam and Muhammad

BEFORE YOU READ

In this lesson, you will learn about the Prophet Muhammad and the beliefs and practices of Islam.

AS YOU READ

Use this diagram to take notes about the life of Muhammad, the beliefs of Islam, and the sources of Islamic authority. Answering the questions at the end of each section will help you fill the chart.

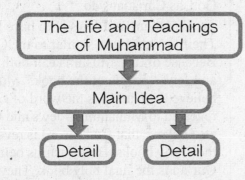

The Life and Teachings of Muhammad

↓

Main Idea

↓ ↓

Detail   Detail

TERMS & NAMES

- **Islam** Monotheistic religion based on the teachings of Muhammad
- **Muslim** Follower of Islam
- **Hijrah** Muhammad's migration from Mecca to Yathrib (Medina)
- **Qur'an** Muslim holy book, which contains God's revelations to Muhammad
- **Sunnah** Islamic guide for proper living, based on the words and deeds of Muhammad
- **mosque** Building used for Muslim worship

The Life and Teachings of Muhammad

(pages 93–94)

Why did Muhammad spread Islam?

Muhammad was born in A.D. 570. He was orphaned as a child and had to work in the caravan trade. He married at the age of 25. Eventually, Muhammad became a successful merchant.

At about the age of 40, Muhammad's life changed. He spent time praying on nearby Mount Hira. One day, he thought he heard the Angel Gabriel call to him. The angel said, "You are the Messenger of God." Soon Muhammad began preaching that there was only one God (Allah in Arabic). He also taught that all other gods must be rejected. People who agreed with this basic belief of **Islam** were called **Muslims.**

Muhammad's preaching had little success at first. So, in 622, he left Mecca with some supporters. They moved to the town of Yathrib. Yathrib was 200 miles north of Mecca. This

move is called the **Hijrah.** Later, Muhammad's followers renamed the town Medina. There, Muhammad's teachings won many converts.

Muhammad and 10,000 of his followers returned to Mecca. They forced the city to surrender. Muhammad then went to the shrine known as the Ka'aba. He dedicated the shrine to Allah.

Muhammad was a strong religious leader. He was also a talented political and military leader. In Medina, Muhammad united his followers with the town's other Arabs and the Jews. Later, Muhammad made treaties of alliance with nomadic tribes. He used his military abilities to spread Islam. Muhammad died in 632. By this time, he had unified much of the Arabian peninsula under Islam.

1. How did Muhammad's life change at about the age of 40?

_____

_____

CHAPTER 3

READING STUDY GUIDE CONTINUED

Islamic Beliefs, Practices, and Law

(pages 94–95)

How do the teachings of Islam provide laws and guidelines for religious practice and everyday life?

Muslims find guidance on how to live their lives in two sources of authority. Those sources are the **Qur'an** and the **Sunnah.**

The main teaching of Islam is that there is only one God, Allah. Muslims believe that the Angel Gabriel revealed God's will to Muhammad. Muhammad taught his followers these revelations. After he died, his followers collected the revelations in a book. This book is the Qur'an, the Muslim holy book.

Muslim's believe that part of Muhammad's mission was to receive these revelations. Another part of his mission was to show how to apply them to life. Muhammad achieved this goal through his words and deeds. These words and deeds are recorded in a book called the Sunnah. Muslims use the Sunnah as a guide for proper living.

Scholars later organized the guidelines found in the Qur'an and Sunna into a system of law. These laws allow Muslims to apply the will of God to their daily lives.

Muslims follow the Five Pillars of Islam. The Five Pillars are duties that Muslims must perform to show their submission to God's will. Muslims also follow the Five Pillars of Islam to serve their community.

Other Islamic customs and laws affect daily lives. Believers are forbidden to eat pork. They are also forbidden to drink alcoholic beverages. Community worship takes place on Friday afternoons. Those who are able gather at a **mosque** to worship.

2. What are the Five Pillars of Islam?

_____

_____

_____

Connections to Judaism and Christianity

(pages 95–96)

What are the connections between Islam, Judaism, and Christianity?

Muslims trace the beginnings of their religion to Abraham. They believe he was a prophet of God. Jews and Christians also believe that Abraham was a prophet. To Muslims, Allah is the same God that is worshipped by Christians and Jews. But Muslims view Jesus as a prophet. They do not view Jesus as the son of God, as Christians do.

Christians and Jews both have holy books. Their teachings are similar to the Qur'an. Because of this, Muslims call both Christians and Jews "people of the book." Muslims believe the Qur'an is the word of God, as revealed to Muhammad. Jews and Christians also believe that God's word is revealed in their holy books. But Muslims believe that the Qur'an is the final holy book. They also think that Muhammad is the last prophet. All three religions believe in heaven, hell, and a final judgment day. Muslim law states that Muslims should tolerate the Jewish and Christian religions.

3. How do Muslims view the Qur'an?

_____

_____

_____

CHAPTER 3

Lesson 3 Islam After Muhammad's Death

BEFORE YOU READ

In the last lesson, you read about the Prophet Muhammad and Islam. In this lesson, you will learn how the Islamic Empire expanded and was governed after Muhammad's death.

AS YOU READ

Use this timeline to take notes about the expansion and rule of the Islamic Empire. Answering the question at the end of each section will help you fill in the chart.

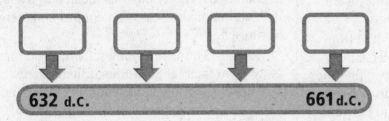

632 d.C.   661 d.C.

TERMS & NAMES

- **caliph** the highest religious and political leader in a Muslim government
- **Shi'a** Muslim group that believed the caliph should be always be a relative of the Prophet Muhammad
- **Sunni** Muslim group that accepted the Umayyads and the rule of elected caliphs

New Muslim Leaders Emerge

(pages 99–100)

Who were the leaders who spread Islam after Muhammed's death?

Muhammad spread Islam across the Arabian Peninsula for more than 20 years. He had begun to establish an Islamic Empire. Then, in June 632, Muhammad died. Muslims were suddenly without a leader.

Muhammad had not named a successor. A successor is a person who replaces another person in an office or position. He also had not told his followers how to choose a successor. The Muslim community selected Abu-Bakr as Muhammad's successor. Abu-Bakr was respected for his devotion to Muhammad and to Islam.

In 632, Abu-Bakr became the first **caliph,** or "successor." Soon some clans on the Arabian Peninsula abandoned Islam. Others refused to pay taxes. A few individuals even declared themselves prophets. But Abu-Bakr reunited the Muslim community by using military force. He brought central Arabia

under Muslim control. He also started to conquer lands to the north. Abu-Bakr ruled only for two years.

1. What two major events happened in the Muslim community in 632?

_____

_____

First Four Caliphs

(pages 100–101)

How did the caliphs who expanded the Muslim Empire treat those they conquered?

Abu Bakr and the next three caliphs had known Muhammad. They used the Qur'an and Muhammad's actions to guide them. Because of this, they are known to some Muslims as "rightly guided" caliphs. Their rule was called a caliphate.

Abu-Bakr died in 634. Muslims controlled most of Arabia by this time. Umar, the second elected caliph, ruled until 644. His armies conquered Syria and lower Egypt. These regions had been part of the Byzantine Empire. Muslim armies also took territory from the Persian Empire.

The next two caliphs were Uthman and Ali. They completed the conquest of Persia. They also conquered the rest of Southwest Asia and parts of North Africa. By 661, the size of the Islamic Empire had increased nearly four times. This expansion was done through conquest or by treaty.

Muslims saw the military victories as signs of Allah's support. They were energized by their faith. In battle, Muslim armies were disciplined and highly skilled.

The Muslims' success also resulted from weaknesses in the Byzantine and Persian empires. These two empires had been fighting each other for a long time. Their armies were exhausted. Also, the Byzantines and Persians persecuted people who did not support their religions. Persecuted people often welcomed Muslim invaders as liberators.

Many conquered people converted to Islam while under Muslim rule. They liked Islam's message of equality and salvation. There was also an economic benefit to converting. Muslims did not have to pay a poll tax. Muslims let conquered people keep their own religions, if they wished to do so.

Jews and Christians received special treatment because they were "people of the book." This treatment included being able to hold important roles in the Muslim state. But Jews and Christians were not allowed to spread their religion.

2. What regions did Muhammad's successors conquer by 661?

_____

_____

A Split in Islam

(pages 102–103)

How did the issue of choosing leaders divid the Muslims?

In 656, a group of rebels murdered Uthman.

His murder started a civil war. One choice for the next caliph was Ali. He was Muhammad's cousin and son-in-law. Mu'awiyah, a governor of Syria, challenged him. In 661, Ali was assassinated. The system of electing a caliph died with him.

A family known as the Umayyads took power. Mu'awiyah, a member of this family, became caliph. The Umayyads set up a hereditary dynasty. This meant that rulers would come from one family. The Umayyads also moved the Muslim capital from Medina to Damascus. Damascus was located in Syria. Its location made it easier to control conquered territories.

Arab Muslims felt Damascus was too far away from their lands. Some of them were also upset about the Umayyads' lifestyle. The Umayyads had abandoned the simple life of previous caliphs. Instead, they had surrounded themselves with wealth. These actions divided Muslims. The actions of the Umayyads also raised questions about how a leader should be chosen.

Most Muslims wanted peace. So they accepted the Umayyads' rule. But a minority resisted. They believed that the caliph should always be a relative of the Prophet. This group was called **Shi'a,** meaning the "party" of Ali. Its members were called Shiites. Those who accepted the Umayyads and the rule of the elected caliphs were called **Sunnis.** This meant followers of Muhammad's example.

This split in the Muslim community became permanent. It led to the collapse of Umayyad rule.

3. What happened in 661 that greatly changed the governing of the Islamic Empire?

_____

_____

_____

CHAPTER 3

Chapter 3 The Beginnings of Islam

Glossary/After You Read

permanently for a long time; continuously

flock travel in large groups

angel a spiritual being that serves God or acts as God's messenger

will wish, desire, or intention

judgment day day at the end of the world when God judges each person's life

disciplined in strict self-control and well-trained

murder the unlawful killing of one person by another

Terms & Names

A. Circle the name or term that best completes each sentence.

1. People who move from place to place to find water and grazing land for their herds are called _____.

    merchants   nomads   clans

2. A journey to a sacred place is called a _____.

    pilgrimage   meditation   retreat

3. Muhammad's migration from Mecca to Yathrib is known as _____.

    Sunna   Shi'a   Hijrah

4. A building for Muslim worship is called a _____.

    cathedral   mosque   oasis

5. A Muslim group that believed that the caliph should always be a relative of the Prophet is called _____.

    Bedouin   Sunni   Shi'a

B. Write a letter of the name of a person that matches the description.

_____ **6.** a member of the Umayyad family   **a.** Mu'awiyah

_____ **7.** believed by Arabs to have built the Ka'aba   **b.** Muhammad

_____ **8.** the first caliph   **c.** Abu-Bakr

_____ **9.** the last "rightly guided" caliph   **d.** Abraham

_____ **10.** murdered by rebels in 656   **e.** Ali

_____ **11.** spread the religion known as Islam   **f.** Uthman

READING STUDY GUIDE CONTINUED

Main Ideas

12. Why did the Bedouins organize themselves into clans?

_____

_____

13. How was the Arabian Peninsula's location good for trade?

_____

_____

14. Why do Muslims believe that following the Five Pillars of Islam is important?

_____

_____

15. How is Islam similar to Judaism and Christianity?

_____

_____

16. What factors enabled the Muslims to conquer so much territory?

_____

_____

Thinking Critically

17. Forming and Supporting Opinions Do you think Muhammad should have named a successor? Why or why not?

_____

_____

_____

_____

18. Making Inferences Why do you think the Umayyads took control of the Muslim empire? Support your answer with evidence.

_____

_____

_____

CHAPTER 3

Lesson 1 The Expansion of Muslim Rule

BEFORE YOU READ

In Chapter 3, you learned that Muhammad died without appointing a successor. Many groups fought for control. In this lesson, you will read about how the Umayyads won the struggle, built an empire, and expanded Muslim rule.

AS YOU READ

Use a chart like the one below to record key information on the lesson's main ideas.

Umayyad Expansion	Unifying the Empire	Umayyad Downfall

TERMS & NAMES

- **Iberian Peninsula** the southwestern tip of Europe, forming the present-day nations of Spain and Portugal
- **bureaucracy** a system of departments and agencies that carry out the work of government
- **Abd al-Malik** Umayyad caliph who declared Arabic the language of government for all Muslim lands

Expansion Under the Umayyads

(pages 113–114)

What lands did the Umayyads add to the Muslim Empire?

After they took power in 661, the Umayyads conquered lands to the east and west. By the early 700s, they controlled much of Central Asia to the east. They also expanded the empire to the west. By 710 they ruled all of North Africa from the Nile River to the Atlantic Ocean. In 711 they entered the **Iberian Peninsula,** the southwestern tip of Europe forming the present-day nations of Spain and Portugal. Using military force and treaties, they took control of most of the peninsula.

Their conquests stopped there. Attempts to conquer more of Europe failed. Muslim forces were defeated in 732 at the Battle of Tours. This stopped their march into Europe. They retreated back to Spain.

1. How did the Umayyads expand Muslim rule?

_____

_____

_____

_____

READING STUDY GUIDE CONTINUED

Uniting Many Peoples

(pages 114–115)

How did the Umayyads build a united empire?

By the early 700s, the Umayyads had a huge empire that covered many lands. They had to bring together people with different cultures and customs. To govern their empire, the Umayyads introduced a system of government called a **bureaucracy,** or a system of departments and agencies that carry out the work of the government. The Umayyads based their system on the bureaucracy of the Byzantine Empire.

Umayyad caliphs ruled their empire from their capital city of Damascus. They appointed Muslim governors emirs to rule the provinces. These emirs relied on local leaders to help them rule. Involving local leaders helped win support for the Umayyads.

People in different parts of the Umayyad Empire spoke their own languages and used different types of coins. When **Abd al-Malik** became caliph in 685, he made two changes that helped unite the empire. First, he made Arabic the language of government for all Muslim lands. Second, he required all parts of the empire to use the same coins. The new coins had quotations for the Qur'an. The coins united the people of the empire by stressing Muslim beliefs. These coins also made trade easier.

People in the Umayyad Empire were also united by the pilgrimage, or hajj, that many Muslims took to Mecca each year. On the hajj, Muslims from many different places met. They returned home to share with others what they had learned about Arabic culture and Umayyad rule.

2. How did the Umayyads unite the Muslim states?

_____

_____

_____

The Overthrow of the Umayyads

(pages 115–116)

What caused the Muslim Empire to split?

Over time, different Muslim groups within the empire began to oppose Umayyad rule. They felt the Umayyads were too interested in living a fancy life and holding onto power. Many groups believed Umayyad rulers did not take their duties as religious Muslim leaders seriously. By the mid-700s, these groups openly spoke out against Umayyad rule. A group called the Abbasids gained support from other Muslim groups unhappy with Umayyad rule.

By 750, these groups led by the Abbasids seized control of the empire. According to some stories, the Abbasids murdered all but one Umayyad leader. This man, Abd al-Rahman, fled to Spain where he reestablished the Umayyad dynasty. After this the Muslim Empire was permanently divided into eastern and western parts.

3. What problems caused the Umayyads to lose the support of many people in the empire?

_____

_____

_____

_____

Lesson 2 A Golden Age in the East

BEFORE YOU READ

In Lesson 1, you read about the rise and fall of the Umayyads and how the Muslim Empire split into eastern and western sections. In this lesson you will learn about the years of Abbasid rule in the east.

AS YOU READ

Use a cluster diagram like the one below to help you form and support an opinion about Abbasid culture. Use the diagram to record information on Abbasid cultural achievements.

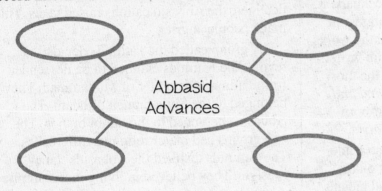

TERMS & NAMES
- **standing army** a fighting force that is maintained in times of peace as well as war
- **Baghdad** city on the Tigris River that became the Abbasid capital in 762
- **golden age** a period during which a country and its culture are at their peak
- **calligraphy** art of fine handwriting
- **Omar Khayyam** Persian-born Muslim poet during the Abbasid period
- **faction** group opposed to the ruling party

Abbasid Rule

(pages 119–120)

How did the Abbasids build a powerful empire?

The main way the Abbasids kept control of their empire was by force. They built a huge **standing army**—a fighting force that is kept in times of peace as well as war. Abbasid leaders put army units at military posts throughout the empire.

They also strengthened and united the empire by including different religious groups in the economic and political life of the empire. All Muslims whether Arab or non-Arab were treated equally. Christians and Jews were encouraged to serve in government.

The Abbasids also strengthened the empire by moving the capital from Damascus to **Baghdad.** The new capital was closer to the area of their most loyal supporters. It was also on old trade routes linking east and west. Baghdad became a major trade center.

Merchants there bought and sold goods not only from all parts of the empire but also from China, India, northern Europe, and Africa.

As trade grew, Baghdad prospered and expanded. By the early 800s, it had more than 900,000 residents. Agriculture and industry thrived. Newly irrigated lands helped farmers grow more crops. Craftsworkers made fine goods sold throughout Europe.

1. How did the Abbasids make sure they held onto power?

_____

_____

Abbasid Advances

(pages 121–123)

What cultural advances did the Abbasids make?

The Abbasids became rich. Some used their wealth to support the arts and learning. In the

READING STUDY GUIDE CONTINUED

800s Muslim culture enjoyed a **golden age.** A golden age is a period during which a country and its culture are at their peak.

During this time, Abbasid artists became famous for beautiful designs in pottery and wood. Their designs were often drawings of plants, flowers, or geometric patterns. Many artists also became skilled at **calligraphy,** or the art of fine handwriting. Calligraphers decorated everything from buildings to books.

During the golden age, Baghdad also became a center of bookmaking and literature. In the 750s, the Abbasids learned to make paper from the Chinese. This advance made it easier to make books and sparked interest in learning. Muslim scholars translated the works of Greek thinkers into Arabic. Muslim writers also created original works. Among the most popular were the tales of *The Thousand and One Nights* and the poems of Persian-born **Omar Khayyam,** author of the *Rubaiyat.*

At this time, Muslim scholars also made advances in mathematics. They built on the ideas of ancient Greeks, Egyptians, and Indians. Al-Khwarizmi drew on Indian ideas to create the Arabic numbering system still used today. Our word *algebra* comes from a set of mathematical calculations he published. The poet Omar Khayyam used his knowledge of mathematics and astronomy to create an accurate calendar.

Muslim scholars also made advances in medicine. A doctor named al-Razi analyzed old medical studies to identify and describe diseases. The Persian doctor Ibn Sina wrote a medical reference book that combined ancient works with recent Muslim discoveries. This book remained a key reference for more than 600 years. The Abbasids also set up hospitals throughout the empire. Unlike most other hospitals at that time, these hospitals treated poor people who couldn't pay.

2. Why is the Abbasid period considered a golden age for Muslim culture?

_____

_____

The Decline of the Abbasids

(pages 124–125)

What problems led to the decline of Abbasid rule?
The Abbasids faced challenges from within and from outside the empire. **Factions,** or opposing groups, within the empire first challenged Abbasid rule in the 800s. They disliked the Abbasid rulers for several reasons. Some Abbasid rulers were fond of easy living. They ignored their government duties. They failed to protect merchants from attacks by robbers. This hurt trade, which was a major source of wealth for the empire. When trade declined, the Abbasid caliphs raised taxes. This made people angrier.

A group called the Fatimids decided to revolt. The Fatimids claimed to be descended from Fatima, a daughter of Muhammad. They belonged to the Shi'a branch of Islam. The Abbasids belonged to the Sunni branch. The two groups had major religious differences. The Fatimids disliked the Abbasids' fancy lifestyle. They believed in living more simply.

In time the Fatimids revolted and drove the Abbasids out of what is today Egypt and Tunisia. They set up their own government, making Cairo their capital. By the late 960s they controlled much of North Africa.

Fighting with the Fatimids and other factions hurt the Abbasids. These problems made them more open to attack by foreigners. In 1055, the Seljuk Turks from Central Asia captured Baghdad. A Seljuk leader became the ruler of the empire. He allowed the Abbasid caliph to stay on as religious leader.

In time, the Seljuks converted to Islam. They expanded the lands under their control and captured Jerusalem. In 1258 a warrior tribe called the Mongols captured and destroyed Baghdad. They killed the Abbasid caliph, ending Abbasid rule and the Seljuk-Abbasid Empire.

3. Why did Abbasid rule end?

_____

_____

CHAPTER 4

Lesson 3 Muslim Rule in Spain

BEFORE YOU READ

In Lesson 1 you read about how, after the Abbasids took power, Umayyad leader Abd al-Rahman escaped to Spain. In this lesson you will learn how Abd al-Rahman and his successors built a new Umayyad kingdom on the Iberian Peninsula.

AS YOU READ

Use a chart like the one below to note the issues and problems that Abd al-Rahman III faced when he came to power and how he responded to them.

Issues and Problems	Responses
Internal revolts	
Attacks from Christian forces to the north	
Threats from North Africa	

TERMS & NAMES

- **al-Andalus** Muslim Spain
- **Córdoba** capital of the Umayyad kingdom on the Iberian Peninsula
- **Abd al-Rahman III** ruler of Muslim Spain during whose reign Al-Andalus reached the height of its power
- **mercenary** soldier paid to fight

The Return of the Umayyad

(pages 131-132)

How did the Umayyads create a strong Muslim kingdom on the Iberian Peninsula?

When Abd al-Rahman came to Spain, he united the many Muslim groups fighting for control. Then he attacked and defeated the ruling factions. In 756 he declared himself ruler of **Al-Andalus,** Muslim Spain. He made **Córdoba** the capital of his kingdom. When news of his success reached Abbasid lands to the east, many Muslims loyal to the Umayyads came to Spain. Their support gave Abd al-Rahman greater control of the government and army. By the time he died in 788, the kingdom of al-Andalus was strong and united.

The kingdom reached the height of its power during the rule of **Abd al-Rahman III.** He strengthened Umayyad rule by overcoming internal revolts and attacks by Christian forces. He kept firm control by building a strong bureaucracy and a huge standing army. Many of his fighters were non-Muslims. They were **mercenaries,** or soldiers paid to fight.

1. What changes did the Umayyads bring to Spain?

_____

_____

_____

READING STUDY GUIDE CONTINUED

The Glory of Córdoba

(pages 132–133)

How did Cordoba become a thriving economic and cultural center under the Umayyads?

By 1000, Córdoba was the largest city in Western Europe. The city's growth was based on its thriving economy. Under Umayyad rule, the city became a center of industry and trade. Craftsworkers in the city's workshops produced silk, leather, carpets, and other goods. Merchants sold these goods throughout Europe and as far away as Central Asia and India. Farming flourished in the countryside around the city.

During the 1000s and 1100s Córdoba also became a major center for culture and learning. It had libraries with thousands of books. Muslim scholars translated many books into Latin. In time, Christian scholars in other parts of Europe read these books. The city's leaders encouraged respected Muslim scholars from Baghdad to come to al-Andalus. They brought fresh ideas and new ways of learning.

2. What made Córdoba a great city during Umayyad rule?

_____

_____

_____

_____

A Golden Age in the West

(pages 134–137)

What cultural developments took place during the golden age in al-Andalus?

A golden age of culture developed in al-Andalus in the 1000s and 1100s. Scholars made key contributions to mathematics, astronomy, geography, medicine, and philosophy. They used mathematics to create accurate calendars. In astronomy, they created tables to show where the planets were located at various times of the year. They also built instruments to view the skies and a planetarium with planets that moved.

A scholar named al-Idrisi contributed to the study of geography. In 1154 he completed an encyclopedia of geographic knowledge with maps and descriptions of many world regions.

In medicine, doctors in al-Andalus wrote medical studies on relations between doctors and patients and on ways to treat diseases. In the late 900s, a doctor named al-Zahrawi wrote a medical encyclopedia on everything from surgery to the care of teeth. Ibn Rushd, another doctor, contributed to philosophy. His studies of Greek thinkers Plato and Aristotle were translated into Latin. They helped reintroduce Greek philosophy to Europe.

Under Umayyad rule, Jews in Spain were welcomed, not persecuted. They contributed greatly to the golden age in al-Andalus. Some held high government offices or acted as advisers to Muslim rulers. The brilliant Jewish scholar Maimonides made contributions to the understanding of science, medicine, religion, and philosophy.

By the early 1200s, the golden age had ended. Different factions fought for control of al-Andalus. Other groups broke away and formed their own smaller kingdoms. In time, Christian forces slowly regained control of the Iberian Peninsula.

3. Why are the 1000s and 1100s a golden age in Al-Andalus?

_____

_____

_____

_____

CHAPTER 4

Chapter 4 The Rise of Muslim States

Glossary/After You Read

stronghold a place that is heavily defended

launch to begin or start

far-flung wide-ranging, extensive

prominent high-ranking, widely known

station assign to a location or position

sugar cane a tall grass with thick, juicy stems from which sugar is produced

script the hand-written letters or symbols of a language

fond having a liking for

loyalist someone who is faithful, especially to a government or leader

pave cover with a hard surface, such as stone, concrete, or asphalt

practical having a useful purpose

diet the usual food and drink consumed by a person or animal

Terms & Names

A. If the statement is true, write "T" on the line. If it is false, write "F" on the line and change the underlined word or words to make it true.

_____ **1.** The Iberian Peninsula is the southwestern tip of Europe where Spain and Portugal are today.

_____ **2.** Mercenaries helped Umayyad ruler Abd al-Rahman III build a strong standing army.

_____ **3.** A purple patch of Muslim culture occurred in Baghdad during Abbasid rule.

_____ **4.** The Fatimids were one of the factions who contributed to the decline of the Abbasids.

_____ **5.** Muslim artists during Abbasid rule became known for mosaics, the art of fine handwriting.

B. Write the letter of each name next to the description that fits it best.

_____ **6.** City on the Tigris River that became the Abbasid capital

_____ **7.** City on the Iberian Peninsula that became the capital of the Umayyad kingdom in Spain

_____ **8.** Ruler of Muslim Spain during the height of its power

_____ **9.** Muslim poet and mathematician during Abbasid rule

_____ **10.** Ruler who helped unite the Umayyad Empire by making Arabic the common language of government

a. Córdoba

b. Omar Khayyam

c. Abd al-Rahman III

d. Abd al-Malik

e. Baghdad

READING STUDY GUIDE CONTINUED

Main Ideas

11. How did the Umayyads build a united empire?

_____

_____

12. What caused the Muslim Empire to split?

_____

_____

13. What were some of the achievements in literature and medicine during the golden age of Abbasid rule?

_____

_____

14. Why did the Abbasids lose control of their empire?

_____

_____

15. What helped Córdoba become a thriving economic and cultural center during Umayyad rule?

_____

_____

16. How did scholars in al-Andalus contribute to geography and medicine?

_____

_____

Thinking Critically

17. Understanding Cause and Effect Why was a common language so important to building the Abbasid Empire?

_____

_____

18. Making Inferences Why do you think Abbasid and Umayyad rulers allowed non-Muslims to participate in government?

_____

_____

Lesson 1 West African Culture and Daily Life

BEFORE YOU READ

In this lesson, you will learn about daily life, the development of the economy, and the oral tradition in early West Africa.

AS YOU READ

Use this chart to take notes about the main sections in this chapter. Answering the questions at the end of each section will help you fill in the chart.

Section	Summary
Village life in West Africa	
Trade and regional commerce	
The oral tradition in West Africa	

TERMS & NAMES

- **kinship** a connection among people by blood, marriage, or adoption
- **clan** a group formed by kinship groups with a common ancestor
- **labor specialization** when people in a society focus on specific types of work
- **griot** a West African storyteller

Village Life in West Africa

(pages 151–152)

What role did families play in West African society?

From 300 to 1500, powerful empires controlled much of West Africa. Most West Africans dealt with their ruler only for court cases and taxes. Many of these people felt a strong loyalty to their village and family.

Family relationships were very important in West Africa. **Kinship** groups formed the government of many African societies. These groups were equal in power. A council of the kinship groups' eldest members often made the decisions. Kinship groups with a common ancestor often formed larger groups called **clans.** Clan members usually followed the same rules.

In West African villages, the way of life for most people centered on farming. Women prepared food and cared for children. They also made pottery and worked in the fields. Men looked after large animals, such as cattle.

They also cleared land for farming and built houses and fences. Children often gathered firewood. In addition, they helped their fathers and mothers.

Some people focused on specific types of work such as farming or trading. This is called **labor specialization.** Labor specialization led to a diverse West African economy. Most people practiced an economy based on farming. Others focused on herding animals or metalworking. Iron technology allowed Africans to create stronger agricultural tools and weapons. As a result, they became wealthier. Also, their population grew. Finally, some people traded goods within West Africa. They also traded with other regions, such as North Africa.

1. What types of work did West Africans specialize in?

_____

_____

Trade and Regional Commerce

(pages 152–153)

How did trading develop in West Africa?

By A.D. 300, population growth and trade had led to the development of West African cities. Gold mining and trade in slaves led to more contact with North Africa. Local and international trade increased. As a result, the cities became more important centers of trade. They also became centers of politics, religion, and education.

Trade between West and North Africa continued to grow. West Africans received salt, cloth, and metal wares from Arab traders. In return, West Africans provided gold, slaves, ivory, and cattle hides.

West African societies gradually developed complex trade systems. Soon kings arose in West African societies. The king kept trade running smoothly. As a result, many people were loyal to him. In addition, kings often played an important role in religion. They were expected to help the economy by performing prayers and rituals.

2. What was the relationship between kings and trade in West Africa?

_____

_____

_____

The Oral Tradition in West Africa

(pages 153–154)

What is oral history?

For centuries, West Africans had no written language. Because of this, they did not record their history in written form. West Africans passed on their history through a collection of stories. These stories were about people and spiritual forces in the natural world. The storytellers were called **griots.** They often used music in their stories.

The stories entertained and educated. The griots passed on a clan's or kinship group's history. West Africans believed their departed ancestors watched over them. They thought that their ancestors could help the living communicate with the creator of the universe. During religious rituals, West Africans appealed to ancestors for favor and protection. Griots often took part in these rituals.

Griots sang for kings, other powerful people, and common villagers. Griots acted out various characters in a story. The audience often participated. Griots are still an important part of West African culture.

3. With no written language, how did early West Africans pass on their history?

_____

_____

_____

_____

Lesson 2 The Empire of Ghana

BEFORE YOU READ

In this lesson, you will learn about the development of the trans-Saharan trade, and the growth and decline of Ghana's empire.

AS YOU READ

Use this chart to take notes about how the people of West Africa built empires from the wealth gained by trade. Answering the question at the end of each section will help you fill in the chart.

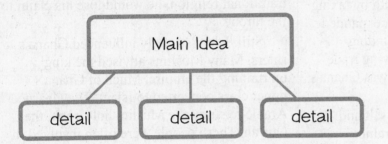

TERMS & NAMES

- **vegetation zone** a region that has certain types of plants
- **Sahara** a large desert of northern Africa
- **savannah** a grassland in a tropical region
- **Ghana** a region between the Sahara and southern West Africa that developed into an empire
- **Almoravids** a group of Muslim Arabs that came to power in North Africa during the 11th century

West Africa's Geography Fuels Empires

(pages 157–158)

What are the three vegetation zones in West Africa?

West Africa's geography helped people develop a strong trade. West Africa has three **vegetation zones:** desert, grasslands, and forests. Soil and climate determine what plants grow in a vegetation zone. For example, a desert has a dry climate. Only plants that use little water grow there.

The northern section of West Africa is part of a large desert. This desert is called the **Sahara.** The middle section of West Africa is a **savannah.** It is flat, grassy, and has scattered trees. Forests make up the southern region of West Africa. The Niger River runs across West Africa. For centuries, the river has been used for transportation and communication. It has also served as a trade route.

The Sahara has rich deposits of salt. Crops, such as millet, grow well on the savannah. The southern forests hold large amounts of gold.

People in the savannah and forests of West Africa had gold, but they wanted salt. People in North Africa had salt, but they wanted gold. As a result, a trans-Sahara trade of gold and salt developed. Trans-Sahara means across the Sahara. People in the Sahara would mine salt. Then they traded it for the gold mined in the forests of West Africa.

Around A.D. 300, savannah and forest people began to use camels to transport goods. Camels could cover great distances with little food or water. These qualities made camels ideal for carrying goods across the Sahara. Traders used camels in groups called caravans. Camel caravans helped increase trans-Sahara trade.

1. What trade goods are found in the different vegetation zones?

_____

_____

_____

READING STUDY GUIDE CONTINUED

The Growth of Ghana's Empire

(page 159)

What, besides goods, can trade bring to a region?

The region between the desert and the forest of West Africa came to be called **Ghana.** The northern part of Ghana became a center of trade. Salt and other goods arrived there after crossing the Sahara. Gold, enslaved people, and goods reached Ghana from the south. The people of Ghana supervised the trading.

The king of Ghana gained wealth by taxing the trade. Using this wealth, Ghana expanded into an empire. It conquered surrounding lands. Cities in Ghana became thriving trade centers. The city of Koumbi Saleh was Ghana's capital.

Most of the people who traded salt and other goods from the north were Arabic speaking Berbers. Most Berbers practiced the religion of Islam. Berber traders brought more than just goods to West Africa. They also introduced their written language (Arabic) into West Africa. In addition, Arabs brought Islam to West Africa.

2. How did Ghana gain wealth?

_____

_____

_____

Islam and Ghana

(pages 160–161)

In what ways did Islam influence Ghana?

Most of Ghana's common people kept their traditional beliefs. Some of Ghana's kings converted to Islam. Even so, they still practiced their traditional religion. According to this religion, kings were descended from the ancestors who settled Ghana. This ancestry gave the king the right to rule. Most people accepted this belief. So if the king rejected the traditional religion, he would lose his claim to the throne.

Still, Islam strongly influenced Ghana's rulers. Many Muslims advised the king on running the empire. Much of Ghana's upper class converted to Islam. They learned Arabic to study the Muslim holy book, the Qur'an. These people were often involved in government. As a result, Islamic beliefs about what is right and wrong influenced Ghana's legal system.

Islam's influence, however, could not stop Ghana's decline. The **Almoravids** came to power in North Africa during the 11th century. They were a group of Muslim Arabs. The Almoravids wanted other Muslims to follow their own view of Islam. In addition, the Almoravids were poor camel herders. Because of this, they did not gain much wealth in trans-Saharan trade. As a result, they envied the great wealth of Ghana. Soon the Almoravids declared war on Ghana. The war weakened Ghana's trade network. Before long, Ghana began to crumble. In 1076, the Almoravids seized the capital city of Koumbi Saleh.

3. Why did the Almoravids declare war on Ghana?

_____

_____

_____

_____

Lesson 3 The Empire of Mali

BEFORE YOU READ

In this lesson, you will learn about the growth and decline of the Mali and Songhai empires.

AS YOU READ

Use this chart to take notes about the similarities and differences between the Mali and Songhai empires. Answering the questions at the end of each section will help you fill in the chart.

	Mali	Songhai
Trade		
Religion		
Decline		

TERMS & NAMES

- **Mali** a West African empire that thrived from about 1240 to the 1400s
- **Sundiata** chief of the Malinke people, established the Empire of Mali
- **Timbuktu** West African city that developed into a center of trade and culture during the 1200s.
- **Mansa Musa** king of Mali's empire from 1312 to 1332
- **Songhai** West African empire that thrived from the mid-1400s to the late 1500s
- **Askia Muhammad** king of the Songhai Empire from 1493 to 1528

CHAPTER 5

Mali Builds on Ghana's Foundation

(pages 165–166)

How could Mali build on Ghana's empire?

The empire of **Mali** was formed around 1240. It was located in the southern area of what had been Ghana's empire. The Malinke people founded the empire of Mali. A great chief named **Sundiata** led the Malinke.

In 1240, Sundiata and his army captured the former capital of Ghana. He expanded his empire beyond Ghana's old border. Sundiata also reestablished the gold-salt trade and expanded trade routes.

Sundiata developed the city of **Timbuktu** as a center of trade and culture. He also supported the development of food crops, cotton farming, and cotton weaving. Sundiata balanced his Islamic belief with his traditional religious beliefs. In this way, he was similar to the kings of Ghana.

After Sundiata's death, the rulers of Mali continued to expand the empire. In 1312,

Mansa Musa became king of Mali. He was a devoted Muslim. He allowed his subjects to practice other religions.

In 1342, Mansa Musa began a pilgrimage to Mecca. On his pilgrimage, he brought 12,000 slaves, 80 camels, and 300 pounds of gold with him. Mansa Musa's pilgrimage greatly impressed those who saw it. It also increased trade for Mali. More merchants wanted to travel to the empire of Mali.

Mansa Musa brought with him an architect and Arab scholars on his return trip to Mali. The architect designed the Sankore mosque in Timbuktu. The scholars taught history, theology, and law in Timbuktu.

Mansa Musa continued to expand the empire until his death around 1332.

1. How did Sundiata improve Ghana's trade?

_____

_____

CHAPTER 5

Decline of Mali

(pages 166–167)

How did weak rulers lead to Mali's decline?

The descendants of Mansa Musa argued about who should be the next ruler of Mali. This internal fighting greatly weakened the empire. Eventually, Timbuktu was raided and burned.

Newly conquered regions of Mali's empire began to rebel. In the east, the **Songhai** people gradually gained strength. Led by the Songhai, the city of Gao declared its independence from Mali in 1400.

In the north, Berber nomads seized much of Mali's territory. They captured Timbuktu in 1431. In the south, bandits began to raid trading caravans and military outposts.

By 1500, rebels and invaders had greatly reduced Mali's territory. Mali was no longer a strong empire.

2. What external factors led to Mali's decline?

_____

_____

_____

_____

The Empire of Songhai

(pages 167–169)

What happened to the Songhai Empire?

During the first half of the 1400s, the Songhai were unsuccessful in forming a strong kingdom.

Since 1431, the Berbers had controlled Timbuktu. In 1468, Muslim leaders asked the Songhai king, Sunni Ali, to help overthrow the Berbers. Sunni Ali agreed. He captured Timbuktu and drove out the Berbers. He also killed many people who lived in the city. Soon Sunni Ali became known as a powerful, harsh leader. He went on to conquer neighboring lands.

Sunni Ali died in 1492. His son was declared ruler. But a leader named **Askia Muhammad** wanted to seize the throne. He and his followers had felt that Sunni Ali did not practice Islam correctly. In 1493, Askia Muhammad defeated Ali's son. He them became ruler of the Songhai Empire.

Askia Muhammad conquered the salt mines to the north. He also expanded Mali's other borders. Soon, the Songhai Empire covered an area larger than the empire of Mali had.

Askia Muhammad organized the government of this vast empire. He began by dividing Songhai into provinces. He then put a governor in charge of each province. Askia Muhammad also set up an organized tax system.

Under Askia Muhammad's rule, Islam spread throughout the empire. Muslim scholars converted many people in the cities to Islam. In rural areas, Islamic beliefs were often blended with traditional religious beliefs.

Askia Muhammad's son removed his father from the throne. The rulers of Songhai after Askia were weak. Using guns, Moroccan forces captured Timbuktu and Gao in 1591. Soon after that, the Songhai Empire collapsed.

3. How was Islam spread during Askia Muhammad's rule?

_____

_____

Chapter 5 West Africa

Glossary/After You Read

firewood wood used to make fires

ware a good or product for sale

oral spoken, rather than written

millet a grass that is used as hay and has seeds that people can eat

supervise watch over and inspect the actions of others

claim a right to something

theology the study of religion

seize to forcefully take control of something

Terms & Names

A. Circle the name or term that best completes each sentence.

1. A West African storyteller is called a _____.

    troubadour   griot   samurai

2. A connection among people by blood, marriage, or adoption is known as _____.

    kinship   specialization   serfdom

3. A grassland in a tropical region is called a _____.

    cataract   savannah   steppe

4. The West African empire that thrived from about 1240 to the 1400s is known as _____.

    Ghana   Arabia   Mali

5. The West African empire that thrived from 1493 to 1528 is known as _____.

    Morocco   Songhai   Timbuktu

B. Write a letter of the name that matches the description.

_____ 6. declared war on Ghana and seized the city of Koumbi Saleh in 1076

_____ 7. a Malinke chief who help form the empire of Mali

_____ 8. made a pilgrimage to Mecca in 1342

_____ 9. drove the Berbers out of Timbuktu in 1468

_____ 10. organized the government of the Songhai Empire

a. Askia Muhammad

b. Sundiata

c. Sunni Ali

d. Mansa Musa

e. Almoravids

STUDY GUIDE CONTINUED

Ideas

1. How did labor specialization led to a diverse economy in West Africa?

_____

_____

12. What role did kings play in the economy of West Africa?

_____

_____

13. Why did Ghana's kings practice both Islam and their own traditional religion?

_____

_____

14. How did Sundiata help the economy of Mali?

_____

_____

15. What internal factors led to the decline of Mali?

_____

_____

Thinking Critically

16. **Forming and Supporting Opinions** Do you think Ghana would have developed into a powerful empire if the people of Ghana never used the camel? Explain your answer.

_____

_____

_____

17. **Making Inferences** In Songhai's cities, many people converted to just Islam. But in rural areas, people often blended Islamic beliefs with their traditional religious beliefs. Why do you think the response to Islam was different in urban and rural Songhai?

_____

_____

_____

CHAPTER 6 | LESSON 1 The Growth of Coastal Trading Cities

Lesson 1 The Growth of Coastal Trading Cities

BEFORE YOU READ

In Chapter 5, you learned about the region of West Africa. In Chapter 6, you will read about the history and culture of central and southern Africa. This lesson examines the migrations of Bantu-speaking people and the growth of city-states along the east coast of Africa.

AS YOU READ

As you read about coastal and trading cities in Eastern Africa, use a graphic like the one below to list how Islam influenced the region.

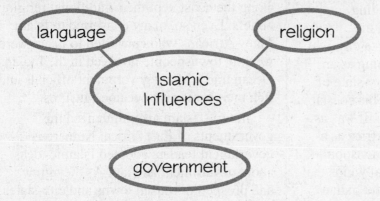

TERMS & NAMES

- **Bantu migrations** historic movement of Bantu tribes from west-central Africa to the south and east
- **Kilwa** wealthy city-state on coast of East Africa
- **Swahili** language that was a blend of Arabic and Bantu

CHAPTER 6

The Land and Its People

(pages 181–182)

How did the Bantu migrations affect southern Africa?

Central and southern Africa have a variety of geographic features. Tropical rainforests cover much of central Africa. Southern Africa has huge grasslands. The people of central and southern Africa are also diverse. They belong to hundreds of different ethnic groups. Many have their own languages, customs, and religions. Many come originally from a single group of African peoples known as the Bantu-speakers.

The first Bantu-speakers lived in west-central Africa. Some time around 1,000 B.C., Bantu tribes began moving south and east through Africa. This movement is called the **Bantu migrations.** It took place over many centuries. About 1,500 years after the migrations began, Bantu-speaking people reached the southern tip of Africa.

As people who spoke Bantu languages moved south and east, they exchanged ideas and intermarried with the groups they met. Such interactions gradually led to the formation of new cultures.

1. What was the result of the Bantu migrations of Bantu-speaking people?

_____

_____

_____

_____

al City-States Emerge

(pages 182–183)

How did Africans and Arabs interact?

By 1100, large numbers of Bantu-speaking peoples had migrated to the eastern coast of Africa. In East Africa, they set up farming villages and trading centers. East African merchants exchanged goods with traders from across the Indian Ocean in India, Persia, and Arabia. Persian traders brought goods made in Asia to Africa. They also brought African raw materials to Asia.

By the 1200s, a network of trading towns and city-states spread along the coast of East Africa. A city-state is a city and its surrounding lands functioning as an independent political unit.) The city-state of **Kilwa** was a key center of trade. This coastal city prospered because its location. It was as far south along the coast of East Africa as a ship from India could sail in one monsoon season. Monsoons are the seasonal winds that blew ships back and forth across the Indian Ocean. To get their trade goods across the ocean, merchants from farther south along the coast of East Africa had to send them to Kilwa where Asian merchants could buy them.

2. What helped Kilwa become rich and powerful?

_____

_____

_____

_____

The Influence of Islam

(pages 183–184)

How did Islam influence culture and government in East Africa?

As trade across the Indian Ocean grew, Arab traders settled in East African port towns. They passed on many aspects of their Arabic culture. Trade between Arabs and Africans led to the creation of a new language, known as **Swahili.** It is a blend of Arabic and Bantu languages. Arabs also introduced the Muslim religion to East Africa. A majority of Africans living along the coast kept their traditional religious beliefs. Even so, many converted to Islam. Many Africans who converted to Islam were wealthy townspeople involved in the Indian Ocean trade. Many government officials and rich merchants also became Muslims.

In time, Islam also influenced the governments of East Africa. Numerous government leaders adopted Islamic ideas about government and law. As they grew and prospered, coastal towns and city-states remained independent. The main reason that these city-states did not join together was that they competed with each other for trade.

3. What influence did Arab traders have on East Africa?

_____

_____

_____

_____

CHAPTER 6 | LESSON 2 Empires Built on Gold and Trade

Lesson 2 Empires Built on Gold and Trade

BEFORE YOU READ
In the last section, you read about the growth of coastal trading cities in East Africa. In this lesson you will read about the rise of the rise and decline of Great Zimbabwe and the Mutapa Empire.

AS YOU READ
Use a graphic like the one below to compare and contrast Great Zimbabwe and the Mutapa Empire.

Great Zimbabwe	Mutapa Empire

TERMS & NAMES
- **Shona** Bantu-speaking people who settled in the valley of the Limpopo River in southern Africa
- **Great Zimbabwe** largest settlement and center of Shona Empire
- **Great Enclosure** largest and most important section of Great Zimbabwe
- **Mutapa** kingdom founded after the fall of Great Zimbabwe

CHAPTER 6

Rise of the Shona Civilization
(pages 13–15)

What was Great Zimbabwe?

By 1000, a Bantu-speaking people called the **Shona** had settled in an area of rich farmland between the Zambezi and Limpopo rivers in southern Africa. They created a thriving empire. The empire was made up of many *zimbabwes,* or settlements surrounded by large stone walls. **Great Zimbabwe** was the largest settlement and center of the Shona empire. The **Great Enclosure** was the largest and most important section of Great Zimbabwe. It contained well-planned brick buildings.

Great Zimbabwe's location and geography helped it grow. Huge plains surrounded the settlement. The Shona farmed and raised cattle on the plains. Great Zimbabwe was also located near key trade routes.

1. How did geography help Great Zimbabwe to grow?

_____

_____

_____

_____

Gold Brings Great Wealth

(page 189)

How did Great Zimbabwe grow rich and powerful?

Great Zimbabwe became rich and powerful from the trade of gold. Gold was one of the main goods traded between Africa and the lands of India and China. Great Zimbabwe did not mine or produce gold. It was, however, located between the gold-producing regions to the west and the trading cities on the eastern coast. Great Zimbabwe grew rich by taxing traders who traveled the trade routes. They demanded gold payments from the region's less powerful leaders.

During the 1400s, Great Zimbabwe began to decline. By 1500 no one lived there. No one knows for sure why people left. Some believe that the overuse of land by cattle and drought caused a shortage of resources. This may have caused people to leave. Others think that people left for better trade opportunities elsewhere.

2. How did Great Zimbabwe gain control of the gold trade?

_____

_____

_____

_____

A New Kingdom Emerges

(pages 190–191)

What empire followed the one at Great Zimbabwe?

As Great Zimbabwe fell, a new empire arose nearby. According to Shona tradition, a man named Mutota from Great Zimbabwe founded this new state. In 1440 he had left Great Zimbabwe and traveled north. He settled in a valley with good soil, rainfall, and wood.

Mutota was a skilled military leader. He used his army to take control of the surrounding area. The people he conquered called him Mutota Mwene Mutapa, or the "Great Pillager." A person who pillages takes things by force. **Mutapa** became the name for both the kingdom and its rulers.

In time, the Mutapa Empire replaced Great Zimbabwe in controlling the gold trade in the region. The Mutapa Empire gained great wealth and power from this trade. In the 1500s, invaders from the European nation of Portugal seized control of the area.

3. How did the Mutapa Empire gain its wealth and power?

_____

_____

_____

_____

Lesson 3 The Kongo Kingdom

BEFORE YOU READ

In this lesson you will read about the Kongo Kingdom in southern Africa and how it was changed by contact with Europeans. You will see how the issue of slavery affected relations between the two groups.

AS YOU READ

As you read Lesson 3, use a chart like the one below to identify the causes and effects of interaction between Kongo and Portugal.

Causes	Effects

TERMS & NAMES

- **Kongo** kingdom on the western coast of Africa
- **Mbanza** capital city of the Kongo kingdom
- **Afonso I** Kongo ruler who spread European influence

A Kingdom Arises on the Atlantic

(pages 195–196)

How did the Kongo kingdom begin?

During the 1300s, a Bantu-speaking people called the Kongo settled along the west coast of southern Africa. They established a kingdom known as **Kongo.** They chose an area near the Congo River because of its fertile soil, good fishing, and nearby deposits of iron and copper ore. They also used the river for trade and transportation. By the 1400s, the Kongo ruled a large area and the land. The center of the Kongo kingdom was its capital city, **Mbanza.**

Kongo rulers set up a well-run government. They created a highly organized kingdom with many levels of government. They divided groups of villages into districts. Districts were grouped together into provinces. The king chose leaders for provinces known as governors. The governors reported to the king. To keep order, the king required all young men to perform military duty at his command.

The king also controlled the Kongo economy. The people mined iron and copper for their own use and for trade. They also made pottery and clothing. The king required the provinces to pay taxes every six months. The provinces often made their payments in cowrie shells, a seashell used for money in Kongo.

1. How was the Kongo kingdom organized?

_____

_____

_____

Kongo and Portugal

(pages 196–197)

How did interaction affect Portugal and Kongo?

In the 1400s, an age of exploration began in Europe. Ships from European nations sailed the oceans exploring new lands. One of the first nations to engage in overseas exploration was Portugal. Portugal was located west of Spain on the Atlantic Ocean. In the early 1480s explorers from Portugal sailed down the western coast of Africa to the Kongo kingdom.

The meeting between the Portuguese and the Kongo people greatly changed the economy, religion, and politics of Kongo. At first, Kongo and Portugal had friendly relations. Kongo traded copper, iron, and ivory to the Portuguese. In return, the kingdom received guns, horses, and other manufactured goods. The Portuguese also introduced the Christian religion and sent missionaries to Kongo. Missionaries are people who travel to other lands seeking followers for their religion.

In 1506, Nzinga Mbemba became ruler of Kongo. During his reign, Portuguese influence in Kongo increased. The new king took the European name **Afonso I.** He copied many Portuguese ways. Afonso made Roman Catholicism the official religion of Kongo. He gave the capital Mbanza a Portuguese name, Sao Salvador. He changed Kongo's political system to reflect European traditions. He created dukes and counts and required them to wear western clothing. He learned to read and write Portuguese and sent many Kongo people to school in Portugal.

2. Name one way that Afonso increased Portugal's influence in Kongo?

_____

_____

_____

_____

Kongo and the Slave Trade

(pages 198–199)

How did the slave trade affect Kongo?

Friendly relations between Kongo and Portugal did not last. The two groups grew apart over the issue of slavery. Early in their trading relationship, Kongo began supplying Portugal with enslaved Africans for use in Portuguese colonies. In return, Kongo's rulers received European goods. Over time, Portuguese demand for African slaves grew greater.

These demands hurt relations between Portugal and Kongo. The growing slave trade began to reduce the population of West Africa. Afonso protested the practice. He urged the Portuguese king to stop. His pleas had no effect. By the time Afonso died in 1543, the Portuguese were enslaving thousands of Africans each year. The slave trade ended relations between Kongo and Portugal. In 1561 Kongo cut itself off from Portugal.

Beginning in the late 1560s, Kongo faced many conflicts. First it went to war with a neighboring kingdom. Then it needed help from Portuguese forces to fight off an invasion by a group called the Jaga. By the early 1600s, the kingdom was stable once again.

3. How did the slave trade affect relations between Kongo and Portugal?

_____

_____

_____

_____

Chapter 6 Central and South Africa

Glossary/After You Read

species group of plants or animals that are able to have offspring

coastal existing along the land next to or near the sea

port place along a body of water where ships can anchor or dock

precious having great value

granite hard rock used in building

resource water, labor, or other supply available for economic development

ample more than enough, plenty

initial happening at the beginning

strained pushed by resentment nearly to open conflict

instability the condition of being unsteady or undependable

Terms & Names

A. If the statement is true, write "true" on the line. If it is false, change the underlined word or words to make it true.

_____ 1. The <u>Bantu migrations</u> were the movement of people who spoke Bantu languages from west-central Africa to southern and eastern Africa.

_____ 2. The settlement of <u>Great Zimbabwe</u> was the center of a Shona empire in southern Africa.

_____ 3. <u>Mutapa</u> was the ruler of Kongo who at first provided slaves for the Portuguese slave trade.

_____ 4. The <u>Great Enclosure</u> was the largest section of Great Zimbabwe.

B. Write a letter of the name that matches the description.

_____ 5. Bantu-speaking people

_____ 6. language that is a mixture of Arabic and Bantu languages

_____ 7. kingdom situated along the Congo River

_____ 8. wealthy East African city-state

_____ 9. capital of the Kongo kingdom

a. Kilwa

b. Shona

c. Mbanza

d. Swahili

e. Kongo

Main Ideas

10. Where did the migrations take the Bantu peoples?

_____

_____

11. Why did coastal city-states in East Africa become important centers of trade?

_____

_____

12. What was the source of wealth and power for Great Zimbabwe?

_____

_____

13. What changes did the trading relationship with Portugal bring to Kongo?

_____

_____

14. What strained relations between the Kongo kingdom and Portugal during Afonso's rule?

_____

_____

Thinking Critically

15. Drawing Conclusions Why do you think the Arabs and Africans in East African port towns developed a common language?

_____

_____

_____

16. Making Generalizations What generalizations can you draw about the Kongo people based on the formation of their kingdom?

_____

_____

_____

Lesson 1 Reunifying China

BEFORE YOU READ

In this lesson, you will learn how the belief systems changed in China after the fall of the Han Dynasty. You will also learn how the Sui and Tang Dynasties reunified China.

AS YOU READ

Use this chart to take notes about the effects of the fall of the Han Dynasty, the spread of Buddhism, and the Sui and Tang Dynasties. Answering the question at the end of each section will help you fill in the chart.

Causes	Effects
The Han Dynasty falls.	
Buddhism becomes widely practiced.	
The Sui and Tang dynasties reunify China.	

TERMS & NAMES

- **nomad** a person who moves from place to place instead of settling permanently
- **Confucianism** a belief system based on the ideas of the Chinese scholar Confucius
- **Buddhism** a religion that is based on the teachings of Siddhartha Gautama
- **Daoism** a belief system that seeks harmony with nature and with inner feelings
- **reunify** to bring a group together after it has been divided

Fall of the Han Dynasty

(page 213)

What happened after the Han Dynasty fell in A.D. 220?

Political struggles and social problems weakened the Han Dynasty. It fell in A.D. 220. China no longer had a single ruler.

Various kingdoms fought among themselves. Invaders from the north crossed into northern China. Floods, droughts, and food shortages also plagued the land.

Despite these troubles, Chinese culture survived. In the north, the invading **nomads**—people who move from place to place—eventually settled down. Gradually, they adopted Chinese customs. In the south, good harvests and growing trade helped people to prosper. Even so, most Chinese people led difficult lives.

1. What were the effects of the fall of the Han Dynasty on China?

_____

_____

Changes in Belief Systems

(pages 214–216)

What changes took place in China's belief systems?

The hardships after the fall of the Han Dynasty led to major changes in China's belief system.

For centuries, the Chinese practiced **Confucianism,** a belief system based on the ideas of Confucius. He taught moral values—ideas of right and wrong. Confucius stressed using right relationships to produce social order. In addition, Confucius focused on education and acting in morally correct ways.

CHAPTER 7

Confucianism affected many aspects of Chinese government. For example, his focus on education helped to produce well-trained government workers. His ideas also influenced society. He thought society should be organized around five basic relationships. A code of conduct governed these relationships. Some of these relationships were based on the family. Confucius wanted children to have respect for their parents and older generations.

Around A.D. 200, the Han Dynasty began to lose power. As this happened, Confucianism began to lose its influence. During this time, many Chinese turned to **Buddhism,** a religion that started in India. Buddhism teaches that people suffer because they are too attached to material things and selfish ideas. It also claims that people can escape suffering by living in a wise and moral way.

Over time, Buddhism spread to China and later to Japan and Korea. Buddhism helped people endure the suffering that followed the fall of the Han Dynasty.

Daoism began in China in the 500s B.C. Daoism is a belief system that seeks harmony with nature and inner feelings.

In the A.D. 600s, Confucianism enjoyed a rebirth. But Confucian thought began to change. Confucian thinkers blended aspects of Buddhism and Daoism into Confucianism. This new Confucianism was more concerned with human behavior.

2. How did China's belief systems change?

_____

_____

The Sui and Tang Dynasties Reunify China

(pages 216–219)

How did the Sui and tang dynasties reunify and strengthen China?

After the fall of the Han Dynasty, the Chinese suffered more than 350 years of conflict. Finally, the Sui Dynasty (581–618) reunified

China and brought order. **Reunify** means to bring a group together after it has been divided.

Yang Jian founded the Sui Dynasty. He was a general in the army of the Zhou. The Zhou were rulers of northern China. In 581, Yang Jian took power by killing the heir to the Zhou throne. By 589, he had conquered the south and reunified China. He became known as Wendi.

Wendi brought back old political traditions. These traditions reminded the Chinese of their glorious past. Wendi reduced conflict by allowing people to follow their own belief systems. In addition, he began public works projects. For example, he started the building of the Grand Canal. It linked northern and southern China.

Wendi and his successor, Yangdi, raised taxes to pay for all the projects. In time, the Chinese people grew tired of high taxes. They then revolted. As a result, the Sui Dynasty fell after only 37 years.

The Tang Dynasty was established in 618 by Gaozu and his son Taizong. It ruled for nearly 300 years. During this period, China expanded its borders on all sides. Tang emperors based the running of the government on Confucian principles. As a result, the Tang government became one of the most advanced in the world.

In 690, Wu Zhao became empress. She was the only woman to occupy the throne of China. She proved herself a capable leader. Wu Zhao conquered Korea.

Another great Tang emperor, Xuanzong, came to power in 712. He ruled for more than 40 years. During his reign, Chinese literature and art reached great heights.

3. What methods did the Sui and Tang dynasties use to reunify and strengthen China?

_____

_____

_____

Lesson 2 Advances Under the Tang and Song

BEFORE YOU READ

In this lesson, you will learn about the political, economic, cultural, and technological advances made under the Tang and Song dynasties.

AS YOU READ

Use this cluster diagram to note information about the main ideas in the lesson. Answering the question at the end of each section will help you fill in the diagram.

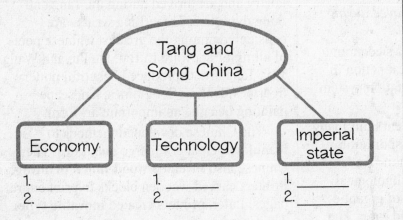

TERMS & NAMES

- **imperial** related to an empire
- **bureaucracy** a government that is divided into departments
- **scholar-official** an educated person with a government position
- **wood-block printing** printing in which a person carved a word or letter on a wooden block, inked the block, and then used it to print on paper
- **movable type** a separate piece of type for each character in a language
- **porcelain** a hard white ceramic often called china

Building the Imperial State

(pages 223–224)

How was the Chinese government organized under the Tang and Song dynasties?

Ruling a large country like China was difficult. To govern better, the Tang rulers developed an imperial state. **Imperial** means related to an empire.

The Tang realized that the Sui had had a well-run government. Because of this, the Tang based much of their government and military organization on Sui models. The Tang also used the Sui tax system.

The Tang government was like a pyramid. An emperor ruled at the top. The emperor's chief advisers served him directly. They were the second-highest level of the pyramid. Below those advisers was the **bureaucracy,** a system of departments and agencies that runs the government. Each department or agency was

in charge of a certain area, such as taxes or the army. Local governments throughout China had to report to this central bureaucracy.

Tang rulers created a new code of law. This new code proved highly effective. China used it from about 624 until the late 1200s.

For many government jobs, people had to take an exam. The state exam tested knowledge of Confucian ideas, poetry, and other subjects. Most people who took the exam failed.

A person who passed the state exam could become a **scholar-official,** an educated person with a government position. Almost all scholar-officials came from the upper class. Only rich people could afford the education needed to pass the test.

After the Tang, the Song Dynasty ruled from 960 to 1279. The Song tried to improve the exam system. It set up more schools. As a result, more people passed the test and got

CHAPTER 7

READING STUDY GUIDE CONTINUED

government jobs. Even so, most officials came from rich families with political influence.

1. What were the features of the Chinese government during the Tang and Song dynasties?

_____

_____

Prosperity from Trade and Farming

(pages 225–227)

On what was China's economy based during the tang and Song periods

Under Tang and Song rule, China's economy grew. China became the wealthiest nation in the world. An improved transportation system contributed to this growth.

The Tang and Song government built many roads and waterways. Better transportation improved trade and communication. Trade was also improved by several technological developments. The development of gigantic ships made sea voyages faster and safer. The magnetic compass also improved travel on the open seas.

Around A.D. 1000, Chinese farmers began planting a new type of rice that farmers could harvest more frequently each year. Soon the food supply expanded. This allowed the population to grow to 100 million.

Soon the people in southern China had more rice than they needed. Having extra food meant that fewer people needed to work as farmers. As a result, more people could work in trade.

The growth of trade led to a rapid increase in the use of money. But large numbers of coins were heavy and difficult to carry. To solve this problem, Tang and Song governments began to print paper money. They were the first governments in history to do so.

As trade increased, more people became merchants. China's merchants lived mostly in cities and towns, where most trade took place. The cities grew and prospered.

2. What brought about the change to a money economy during China's Tang and Song dynasties?

_____

_____

A Time of Brilliant Achievements

(pages 227–229)

What technological advances were made under the Tang and Song dynasties?

Poetry and art thrived during the Tang and Song dynasties. Three Tang writers are considered among the greatest Chinese poets of all time. They are Li Bai, Du Fu, and Wang Wei. Tang artists produced beautiful pottery figurines. During Song times, landscape painting became an important art form.

The Chinese developed methods to manufacture paper in large quantities. The Chinese also invented **wood-block printing.** Printers carved wooden blocks to print entire pages. Later, printers created **movable type.** The Chinese used paper and printing to make the first printed books.

Chinese technology shaped history in many different ways. Papermaking spread west to Europe in the mid-1100s. The Chinese invented gunpowder, which they used for fireworks. Later gunpowder changed warfare. It made deadly new weapons possible. The magnetic compass also spread to Europe. Compasses made the European Age of Exploration possible.

The Chinese influenced daily life by exporting **porcelain,** a hard white ceramic, and tea to the world.

3. What were some key Chinese inventions or products that influenced the world?

_____

_____

CHAPTER 7

Lesson 3 The Mongol Empire

BEFORE YOU READ

In Lesson 1, you read about people from the north who invaded China after the fall of the Han Dynasty. Nearly a thousand years later, as you will read in this lesson, people from the north once again invaded China.

AS YOU READ

Use a diagram like the one below to record the major events of Mongol rule in China.

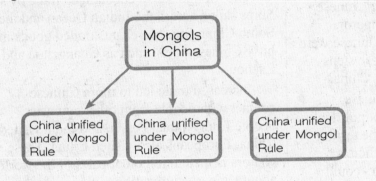

Mongols in China
- China unified under Mongol Rule
- China unified under Mongol Rule
- China unified under Mongol Rule

TERMS & NAMES

- **Genghis Khan** strong Mongol leader who unified the Mongols around 1206 and started an empire that would eventually stretch from northern China to Europe
- **Kublai Khan** grandson of Genghis Khan who took power in 1260 and captured southern China, becoming the first ruler in 300 years to control all of China
- **Mongol Ascendancy** period during which the Mongols controlled China and Central Asia
- **Marco Polo** trader from Venice, Italy, who traveled the Silk Roads to China and worked for Kublai Khan

---

The Mongol Invasion

(pages 233–234)

Who were the Mongols?

The Mongols were a people that lived to the northwest of China. They were nomads. Nomads are people who move from place to place. The Mongols had no central government. Instead, they lived in independent family groups called clans. Around 1206, though, a man named Temujin united the clans for the first time. He became the khan, or ruler, of all Mongol tribes. He took the name **Genghis Khan,** which means "universal ruler."

As nomads, the Mongols had a military advantage over settled people. Settled people had to defend their towns and villages. Nomads could attack quickly and then move on. Using this advantage, Genghis attacked northern China and Central Asia.

Genghis died in 1227. After he died, his son Ogadai took power. Ogadai conquered all of northern China. He also extended the Mongol Empire as far as Russia and Persia. The Mongols divided the empire into four parts. Each part was called a khanate. A different relative of Genghis Khan ruled each khanate.

Kublai Khan took power over the empire in 1260. Kublai was Genghis' grandson. In 1260, the Chinese Song Dynasty still controlled southern China. Kublai defeated the Song in 1279. The Mongols now controlled all of China. They ruled until 1368.

1. By what year did the Mongols conquer all of China?

_____

_____

CHAPTER 7

Mongol Government

(page 237)

What was the Mongol government like?

Kublai Khan was the first ruler in 300 years to control all of China. The Mongols were also the first foreign power to rule China. Kublai ruled for 15 years. He died in 1294.

The Mongols did not have much experience with government. But the Chinese had a lot of experience. Kublai kept some of the Chinese governing traditions. For example, he built his capital at Beijing, using Chinese styles. He also declared himself emperor, beginning the Yuan Dynasty. The Chinese were familiar with such steps. Taking these steps made it easier for Kublai to control China.

However, Kublai did not let Chinese people gain political power. He kept political power for the Mongols. He ended the testing system for choosing government officials. Only Mongols and trusted foreigners could get important positions. The Mongols limited Chinese people to minor jobs with little power.

Kublai Khan was a capable leader. He worked to rebuild China, which had suffered from years of warfare. He also promoted trade and helped to build contacts with other regions.

2. What role did Chinese people play in the Mongol government?

_____

_____

_____

Opening China to the World

(pages 237–239)

What was the Mongol Ascendancy?

Kublai Khan helped make China more open to the outside world. The Mongols encouraged foreign trade. They also welcomed visitors from other countries.

In the past, China had closed overland trade routes because of war and banditry, or stealing. Now, the Mongols controlled Central Asia. Mongol control made the overland routes safe. The period of control is called the **Mongol Ascendancy.** Groups of traders traveled over the **Silk Roads.** These were ancient trade routes between China and the Black Sea. Traders carried silks, ceramics, tea, and other goods to Western markets. Traders returned with new foods, plants, and minerals.

The Mongols also encouraged trade by sea. Ships sailed across the Indian Ocean and the South China Sea. Merchants traded goods in busy Chinese ports, such as Guangzhou and Fuzhou.

Increased trade led to more Chinese contact with people from other countries. People from Arabia, Persia, and India visited China. Europeans also visited China. These visitors helped to tell other parts of the world about Chinese civilization.

The most famous European visitor was Marco Polo. He was a trader from Venice, Italy. He traveled the Silk Roads with his father and uncle. He arrived in China around 1275 and stayed for 17 years. After he arrived, Polo entered the service of Kublai Khan. He traveled around China doing work for the government. Later, he published a book about his travels. The book was a great success in Europe. Even so, many Europeans found some of Polo's stories about China hard to believe.

3. How did China become more open to foreigners?

_____

_____

_____

Lesson 4 A Return to Chinese Rule

BEFORE YOU READ

In this lesson, you will learn how the Chinese regained control of their country. You will also learn about the rule of the Ming and Qing dynasties.

AS YOU READ

Use this web diagram to take notes about the great ocean voyages undertaken during the Ming Dynasty. As you fill in the chart, consider why a country might want to limit contact with the outside world.

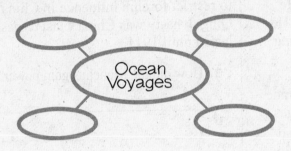

Ocean Voyages

TERMS & NAMES
• **Forbidden City** a group of palaces and temples surrounded by walls in Beijing, China
• **maritime** related to the sea
• **tribute** payment made by one country to another as a sign of respect
• **Zheng He** an admiral of the Chinese fleet who completed seven long voyages between 1405 and 1433
• **Manchus** people who lived in Manchuria and conquered China in 1644

Overthrowing the Mongols

(pages 239–240)

How was the Ming Dynasty established?

Kublai Khan died in 1294. Afterwards, Mongol rule slowly weakened. In 1368, a rebel army led by Zhu Yuanzhang overthrew the Mongol emperor.

Zhu Yuanzhang, under the name Hongwu, became the first emperor of the Ming Dynasty. He set out to bring back China's imperial state. Hongwu encouraged Confucianism. He also brought back the state exams. He rebuilt roads, canals, and irrigation systems. These projects helped trade. He improved China's defenses by rebuilding and extending the Great Wall. Hongwu also helped farmers by lowering taxes. In addition, he provided them with land.

Eventually, Hongwu began to abuse his power. He ended public discussion of policies. Instead, he made decisions in secret. He took control of all government offices. Hongwu also set up a secret service to spy on his people. And he had tens of thousands of people arrested for treason and killed.

Hongwu died in 1398. He had chosen his grandson to succeed him. Not everyone supported this decision. A struggle for power began. It lasted for five years. Finally, a son of Hongwu named Yongle won victory. He declared himself emperor in 1403.

Yongle was a strong, capable leader. The Ming Dynasty reached the height of its power under his rule. Yongle built a new capital city at Beijing. A large group of palaces and temples stood at the center of the city. These buildings were surrounded by 35-foot-high walls. Commoners and foreigners were not allowed to enter this area. As a result, this group of buildings became known as the **Forbidden City.**

1. What improvements did the Ming emperors make in China?

_____

_____

_____

CHAPTER 7

Trade and Overseas Voyages

(page 241)

How did China's relations with the outside world change under the Ming emperors?

In the early 1400s, Yongle built a fleet of ships, which he sent on a series of maritime voyages. **Maritime** means related to the sea. Yongle wanted to extend Chinese influence. He also wanted tribute from other countries. **Tribute** is a payment by one country to another as a sign of respect.

China completed seven long voyages between 1405 and 1433. Admiral **Zheng He** led the fleet. He had as many as 300 ships. He also had nearly 28,000 crew members. Zheng He sailed around Southeast Asia to India, Arabia, and Africa. He returned with tribute that included gold and jewels. China's foreign trade and reputation grew because of these voyages.

By the 1430s, Yongle and Zheng He had died. Most Confucian officials thought China gained little from trade. They also thought that China benefited little from contact with foreigners. These officials were far more concerned with threats of invasions from Central Asia. So the Ming government ended the maritime voyages.

China did not remain isolated. Chinese merchants expanded trade with the rest of Southeast Asia. Also, European ships were traveling to China by the early 1500s. The Chinese traded silk, tea, and porcelain in return for a variety of Western goods, including silver.

2. How did China's policies change after the 1430s?

_____

_____

_____

The Last Dynasty

(page 242)

How was the Qing Dynasty established?

The Ming Dynasty declined after almost 300 years in power. Weak rulers, high taxes, and poor harvests led to rebellion. To the northeast of China was a region called Manchuria. The people there were known as the **Manchus.** In 1644, the Manchus conquered China. They started the Qing Dynasty.

The Manchus allowed only limited trade. They also limited foreign contacts and tried to restrict foreign influence in China. The Qing dynasty was China's last dynasty. It lasted until 1911.

3. How did the Manchus gain power?

_____

_____

_____

Chapter 7 China Builds an Empire

Glossary/After You Read

plagued afflicted, troubled, or annoyed
harmony an agreement in feeling
complex having many connected parts
practical useful in a common activity
figurine a small statue, often made of clay
diplomat a person who represents a government in dealings with other countries
treason helping an enemy of one's own country
symbolize to represent something else

Terms & Names

A. Circle the name or term that best completes each sentence.

1. To _____ means to bring a group together after it has been divided.

> clarify   rectify   reunify

2. A government that is divided into departments is known as a _____.

> bureaucracy   theocracy   monarchy

3. An educated person with a government position is called a _____.

> merchant   artisan   scholar-official

4. The religion based on the teachings of Siddhartha Gautama is known as _____

> Confucianism   Buddhism   Daoism

5. A payment made by one country to another as a sign of respect is known as a _____.

> bounty   tribute   bribe

B. Write the letter of each name next to the description that fits it best.

_____ **6.** overthrew the Mongol emperor in 1368

_____ **7.** an admiral of the Chinese fleet

_____ **8.** means "universal ruler"

_____ **9.** an Italian trader who traveled the Silk Roads to China

_____ **10.** conquered China in 1644

_____ **11.** founded the Yuan Dynasty

a. Genghis Khan
b. Hongwu
c. Kublai Khan
d. Manchus
e. Zheng He
f. Marco Polo

CHAPTER 7

Main Ideas

12. What did the teachings of Confucius stress?

_____

_____

13. The Tang government was like a pyramid. What made up the top-three levels of this pyramid?

_____

_____

14. How did movable type help the Chinese to record their knowledge in a permanent form?

_____

_____

15. How did the Mongols improve trade in China?

_____

_____

16. What was the Forbidden City?

_____

_____

Thinking Critically

17. **Comparing and Contrasting** What were similarities and differences between the Tang and Yuan dynasties?

_____

_____

_____

_____

18. **Forming and Supporting Opinions** Why do you think Hongwu began to abuse his power? Support your answer with evidence.

_____

_____

_____

Lesson 1 Land of the Rising Sun

BEFORE YOU READ

Chapter 7 described China's achievements in technology, government, and thought. This lesson looks at the geography, social system, and government of early Japan. You will also learn about the influence of Chinese culture on Japan.

AS YOU READ

Use a cluster diagram like the one below to record key information about the main ideas in Lesson 1.

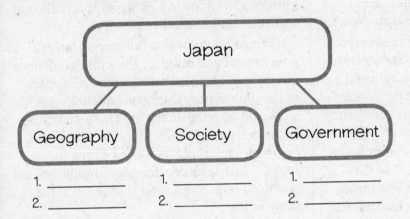

TERMS & NAMES

- **Shinto** Japanese religious tradition based on respect for nature and ancestors
- **regent** Official who rules until a child who will become an emperor or empress is able to rule
- **Prince Shotoku** One of Japan's most important regents
- **embassy** Office of a government in another country

The Effects of Geography on Japan

(pages 251–252)

How was Japan's history influenced by its landforms, climate, and closeness to China and Korea?

The island of Japan is 120 miles off the coast of Asia. In some ways living in Japan is hard. Only 15 percent of the land is flat enough for farming. From time to time, it has earthquakes, tidal waves and hurricanes. It lacks energy resources like coal and oil. But Japan has advantages, too. It has a mild climate with plenty of rain. The ocean provides fish and protection from invasion.

Japanese culture expresses a love for the natural beauty of its mountains and land through **Shinto.** Shinto means "way of the gods." This religion is based on respect for nature and ancestors. Rocks, trees, rivers, and other natural objects are home to divine spirits according to Shinto beliefs.

Korea and China are Japan's closest neighbors. Both influenced its culture, especially China. Chinese beliefs and ideas had an impact on religion, government, arts, and agriculture. Japan's name comes from the Chinese. They called the islands "land of the rising sun," or "jih-pen."

1. How did Japan's location affect its culture?

_____

_____

_____

_____

Early Japanese Society

(pages 252–253)

How was early Japanese society organized?

Early Japan was divided into clans. Clans were families of people related by blood or marriage. Clans fought each other for land because land was the main source of power and wealth. Powerful nobles led each clan. Most of the people were commoners. They lived in villages and farmed or fished. A few were slaves. The Shinto religion helped unite Japanese society. Nobles and commoners honored the same divine spirits and ancestors.

By the 400s, the Yamato clan had become the most powerful clan. Japan's first emperors came from this clan. The Japanese believed members of the Yamato clan were descendents of the sun goddess. Because of this belief, they treated the emperor as both human and divine.

The emperor claimed to rule. But military leaders held the real power. Leaders of the Yamato clan fought each other for this power. Japan had many different military leaders, but it rarely changed emperors.

If a child became emperor or empress, a **regent** was appointed. This official ruled for the child until the child was old enough to take over. One of the most important regents was **Prince Shotoku.**

2. Who held real power in early Japanese society?

   _____

   _____

   _____

   _____

The Reign of Prince Shotoku

(pages 253–254)

What role did Prince Shotoku play in Japan's history?

Prince Shotoku acted as regent for his empress aunt. He ruled from 592 to 622. Shotoku admired Chinese culture. So he brought Chinese culture to Japan. He sent Japanese scholars and artists to China to study Chinese society. He also welcomed skilled Chinese workers to Japan. He opened a Japanese **embassy** in China. An embassy is an office of a government in another country.

Prince Shotoku also influenced Japan's government and religion. He wrote guidelines for Japanese leaders based on the principles of the philosopher Confucius, including hard work and obeying authority. These guidelines became Japan's first constitution. He also helped spread Buddhism from China to Japan. Most Japanese accepted Buddhism and practiced both Shinto and Buddhism at the same time.

3. What was the most lasting effect of Prince Shotoku's reign?

   _____

   _____

   _____

   _____

Lesson 2 Growth of Japanese Culture

BEFORE YOU READ

In Lesson 1, you read about how Japan was influenced by Chinese culture. In this lesson, you will learn how the Japanese adapted foreign customs and ideas to meet their own needs.

AS YOU READ

Use a web diagram like the one below to record information on three categories of Japanese culture and details about them.

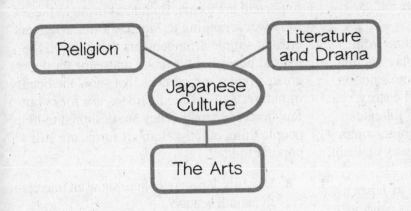

TERMS & NAMES

- **Zen** sect of Buddhism that emphasized self-discipline, simplicity, and meditation
- **noh** a style of drama developed in Japan in the 1300s where actors wear wooden masks
- **kabuki** a style of drama developed in Japan in the early 1600s that combines singing, dancing, and elaborate costumes
- **Lady Murasaki Shikibu** one of Japan's finest writers and author of *The Tale of the Genji.*
- **haiku** a form of poetry with 17 syllables—three lines of 5,7, and 5 syllables

Japanese Forms of Buddhism

(pages 257–258)

How did the Japanese accept Buddhism?

Buddhism began in India. It spread to China and then Korea. It arrived in Japan in the A.D. 500s. Buddhism had a powerful influence on Japanese culture. Many Japanese liked the Buddhist belief that a person could find peace and happiness by leading a life of virtue and wisdom. Over time, different forms, or sects, of Buddhism developed in Japan. In the Tendai sect, members focused on studying texts. In Shingon, they stressed performing certain ceremonies.

Some forms thrived. Others died out. The Japanese adopted the beliefs and practices that best met their needs. Beginning in the 1100s, **Zen** became the most popular form of Buddhism. Zen Buddhists believe self-discipline, leading a simple life, and meditation help a person find inner peace.

Zen influenced Japanese culture in several ways. Samurai practiced it because they thought it would give them inner peace and aid them in battle. The works of some artists were influenced by its simplicity and boldness. In time, Zen spread to other countries and became especially popular in western countries.

1. Why were samurai and artists attracted to Zen Buddhism?

_____

_____

_____

_____

CHAPTER 8

READING STUDY GUIDE CONTINUED

A Golden Age of Literature and Drama

(pages 258–260)

What is unique about Japanese literature and drama?

One of the greatest periods of literature for Japan was the 800s. People today still read diaries, essays, and novels from this time. The Japanese adopted the China's writing system. They used Chinese characters to write Japanese words. Like Chinese, Japanese writing uses characters to stand for things, actions, ideas and certain sounds.

Two unique styles of drama come from Japan—**noh** and **kabuki.** In noh plays, actors wear painted wooden masks to show emotion. Costumes, gestures, and music tell a story. Noh plays often retell legends and folktales. Most actors are men. Kabuki combines singing and dancing with costumes and heavy makeup. Both styles are still popular today.

Lady Murasaki Shikibu, one of Japan's finest writers, lived at the emperor's court in the early 1000s. Her book, The Tale of Genji, tells about the life of a prince in the imperial court. She created the world's first important novel. Until then, Japanese books were either retellings of old myths or collections of stories. Her novel was the first long, realistic story about one person. Japanese poets also created a new type of short poem called a haiku. It has only 17 syllables.

2. What new forms of drama and literature did the Japanese develop?

_____

_____

_____

_____

Distinctive Japanese Arts

(pages 260–261)

What themes are reflected in Japanese arts?

Many Japanese art works expressed the themes of simplicity and love of natural beauty. Calligraphy and brush painting were key art forms. Calligraphy is the art of beautiful writing. Other artists painted with ink on paper scrolls and silk. They created landscapes and pictures of historical events or daily life.

Flower arranging and gardening were other important art forms. Buddhists brought the art of flower arranging to Japan. Flower arrangers created simple arrangements that showed the natural beauty of flowers. Landscape gardeners created parks and gardens that show the beauty of nature. Zen-inspired gardens use rocks but few flowers or trees. They are designed to help people think quietly. Both art forms are still popular today.

3. How did Japanese culture show an interest in natural beauty?

_____

_____

_____

_____

Lesson 3 Samurai and Shoguns

BEFORE YOU READ

As you read in Lesson 1, although an emperor ruled Japan, noble families often held the real power. In this lesson, you will learn how the nobles fought each other to gain power.

AS YOU READ

As you read Lesson 3, record major events in Japan during the age of the samurai and shoguns on a time line like the one below.

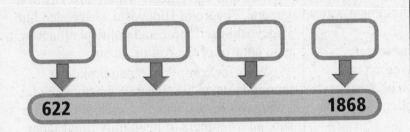

622   1868

TERMS & NAMES
- **daimyo** a large landowner in Japan
- **samurai** a trained warrior who belonged to the private armies of the daimyo
- **vassal** a person who receives land and protection from a lord in return for loyalty
- **shogun** the Japanese military leader who ruled on the emperor's behalf
- **Tokugawa Shogunate** the rule of Japan by Tokugawa Ieyasu and his successors in the Tokugawa family

Nobles Gain Power

(pages 267–268)

How did Japanese nobles gain power?

Japan remained strong and united for some time after Prince Shotoku's rule ended. By the 800s, the Fujiwara family had become the real rulers of Japan. The emperor had little power. The Fujiwaras ruled for 300 years.

In the 1100s, the power of the central government and the Fujiwara family weakened. The government began to run out of money. It also began to lose control over large landholders. As the central government grew weaker, noble families gained power. These large landowners called **daimyo** refused to pay taxes to the government. They had their own private armies of trained warriors called samurai. Each daimyo hired **samurai** to protect their own lands. They also attacked other daimyo armies. The daimyo wanted to gain more land to increase their wealth and power.

Order began to break down in society as the central government lost power.

More robberies, murders, and lawbreaking occurred. Small landowners did not feel safe. They wanted protection. They looked for a more powerful lord, or large landowner, for protection. They agreed to be loyal to this lord and serve in his army in exchange for his protection. A person who gets land and protection from a lord in return for loyalty is called a **vassal.** This new system of local rule increased the power of the daimyo. It marked the start in Japan of feudalism, a system of local rule similar to that in ancient China and medieval Europe.

1. Why did power shift from the central government to the nobles?

_____

_____

_____

_____

READING STUDY GUIDE CONTINUED

The Rise of a Military Society

(pages 268–269)

How did Japan become a military society?

The daimyo gained and held power with the help of their armies. The result was that Japan had a military society for many centuries. Warriors were a key part of this society. Samurai warriors lived by a code of honor called bushido. They were expected to be loyal and brave. They were also expected to fight for their lord even if it meant they could not protect their own families. Zen Buddhism was an important part of their lives.

Women had higher standing in society at this time than at other times. Women in warrior families learned to fight with weapons to protect their families from robbers when the men were away fighting.

The emperor remained in office while the nobles fought among themselves. But he had no real power. Military leaders called **shoguns** controlled the government and ruled the country. Shogun meant "supreme commander of the army." Minamoto Yoritomo became the first shogun in 1192. Japan remained under a shogunate, or military government, for nearly 700 years.

2. How did Japan change when Minamoto Yoritomo came to power?

_____

_____

_____

_____

Three Powerful Warriors Unify Japan

(pages 270–273)

How did powerful military leaders unify Japan?

Three strong military leaders united Japan. They did so by ending the fighting between rival daimyo. The first of these leaders was a daimyo named Oda Nobunaga. His soldiers were the first Japanese army to use guns in battle. He won control of nearly half of Japan by wars and agreements with rivals. His best general, Toyotomi Hideyoshi, succeeded him. Hideyoshi used force and political alliances to gain control of the rest of Japan.

Wars for control of Japan broke out among Hideyoshi's generals when he died. Tokugawa Ieyasu won the wars and became shogun. Members of his family ruled Japan for 250 years. The rule of Ieyasu and others in the Tokugawa family is called the **Tokugawa Shogunate.**

Japan was building ties with Europe when Ieyasu became shogun. Traders and missionaries had brought Western ideas and goods. The Tokugawa shoguns feared these foreign influences might change Japan. So they banned Christianity and all foreigners. They also ended nearly all foreign trade. They even would not let Japanese leave Japan. By the mid-1600s, Japan had become isolated, or separated from the world. This isolation lasted two centuries.

3. What was the result of the struggle to unite Japan?

_____

_____

_____

_____

Lesson 4 Korea and Southeast Asia

BEFORE YOU READ

In Lesson 1, you read that Japan was influenced by Chinese culture. In this lesson, you will learn that Korea and kingdoms in Southeast Asia also borrowed from China, and some also borrowed from India.

AS YOU READ

Use a chart like the one below to compare the accomplishments of the kingdoms discussed in this section.

Korea	Vietnamese Kingdoms	Khmer Empire
1.	1.	1.
2.	2.	2.
3.	3.	3.
4.	4.	4.

TERMS & NAMES

- **Koryo** one of the earliest kingdoms in what became Korea.
- **celadon** a type of pottery often with a bluish-green color
- **Nam Viet** a kingdom of the Viet people
- **Khmer Empire** the most powerful and longest-lasting kingdom in Southeast Asia
- **Angkor Wat** a temple complex of the Khmer Empire and the largest religious structure in the world

---

An Independent Korea

(pages 275–277)

Why did Korea adopt many elements of the culture of China?

Korea developed independently of China. But it was greatly influenced by it. The Koreans borrowed Chinese practices and ideas. They changed them to meet their own needs.

Korea is a peninsula. It extends off the Asian mainland from northern China. Korea is also close to the islands of Japan. Chinese culture sometimes spread to Japan from Korea.

Chinese of the Han dynasty invaded northern Korea in 108 B.C. The Koreans resisted and won back most of the conquered territory by 75 B.C. During the next 700 years, the area was divided into three warring kingdoms. It stayed that way until the Silla Kingdom conquered the other two. The Silla Kingdom ended in 935. A kingdom called **Koryo** replaced it. The modern name Korea comes from this kingdom's name.

The Koreans learned papermaking, printing, and ways to grow rice from the Chinese. They adapted Chinese artistic styles, including a method of making pottery. Korean **celadon**, a type of pottery with a bluish-green color, became famous. Korea also accepted two belief systems from China: Buddhism and Confucianism.

Korea remained independent and united for centuries. But it struggled to stay free of foreign control. The Mongol conquerors of China took control of Korea in the 1200s. They held control until the late 1300s when the Mongol empire in China ended. In 1392, the Yi family started the Choson dynasty. Its rulers stopped an invasion from Japan and ruled Korea for over 500 years.

1. What aspects of Chinese culture did the Koreans adopt?

_____

_____

READING STUDY GUIDE CONTINUED

Vietnamese Kingdoms

(pages 277–278)

What role did China play in the development of Vietnamese kingdoms?

Mountains separate the mainland peninsula of Southeast Asia from China to the north. Chinese soldiers, merchants, and missionaries came by sea or along the coast to Vietnam. They brought Chinese culture to Vietnam and nearby regions.

The Viets were a people who lived just south of China in what is now Vietnam. The country was invaded and influenced by China for much of its history. The Chinese Empire conquered the Viet kingdom called **Nam Viet** in 111 B.C. China's rulers forced the Vietnamese to adopt their culture. They had to speak Chinese and wear Chinese clothes. They forced the Vietnamese to follow two belief systems, Confucianism and Daoism.

Two Vietnamese sisters, Trung Trac and Trung Nhi, led an unsuccessful rebellion against China's rule in A.D. 40. The Vietnamese rebelled several more times over the next few centuries. At the same time they fought the Chinese, they adopted many aspects of Chinese culture. One important aspect was Buddhism. In the early 900s, the dynasty that ruled China weakened. The Vietnamese broke free. They set up an independent kingdom called Dai Viet. In the 1200s, fighting with the Mongols who ruled China weakened the kingdom. Dai Viet finally drove out Chinese invaders in 1428. It then seized Champa, a rival kingdom to the south. This strengthened Dai Viet's position.

2. How was Vietnam shaped by Chinese influences?

_____

_____

_____

The Khmer Empire

(pages 278–279)

How was the Khmer Empire able to prosper between two powerful neighbors—China and India?

The **Khmer Empire** was the most powerful and long-lasting kingdom in Southeast Asia. It was in what is today Cambodia. Its neighbors India and China influenced Khmer culture. The Khmer set up a kingdom on the mainland peninsula in the 500s. It prospered. This was mainly so because farmers had great success growing rice using irrigation systems and better seeds. The Khmer learned rice farming from the Chinese. From India, the Khmer took ideas about rule by a god-king, a writing system, Hinduism, and Buddhism.

Khmer rulers built a new capital at Angkor in the late 800s. Workers constructed a group of temples there known as **Angkor Wat** in the 1100s. This temple complex still exists today. It is the largest religious structure in the world. The Khmer Empire reached its peak in the 1200s. After that time, attacks by neighboring empires weakened it. The empire ended in 1431. It fell to the Thais, a people from what is now Thailand.

3 How was Khmer culture influenced by China and India?

_____

_____

_____

Chapter 8 Japan, Korea, and Southeast Asia

Glossary/After You Read

abundant more than enough; plentiful

lush covered with plant growth

diary written record of a person's thoughts and experiences

syllable word or word part pronounced as a single sound

scroll a roll of parchment or paper on which something is written or painted

pledge to promise

fearsome causing fear

succession pact or process of following in order or sequence

supremacy condition or quality of being supreme

glaze a coating applied to ceramics for baking in a kiln

seed part of a plant that contains the material from which a new plant can grow

Terms & Names

A. If the statement is true, write "true" on the line. If it is false, change the underlined word or words to make it true.

_____ **1.** The <u>Shinto</u> religion came to Japan from China.

_____ **2.** <u>Prince Shotoku</u> helped bring Chinese culture to Japan.

_____ **3.** The <u>Tokugawa Shogunate</u> began the fight to unite Japan by gaining control of half of Japan.

_____ **4.** The Chinese conquered and ruled the kingdom of <u>Nam Viet</u> for a time.

_____ **5.** The economy of the <u>Khmer Empire</u> was built on the skill of its farmers in growing rice.

B. Write the letter of the name or term that matches the description.

_____ **6.** A form of short poem invented by the Japanese

_____ **7.** A Japanese military leader who ruled for the emperor

_____ **8.** Wrote *The Tale of the Genji*

_____ **9.** Introduced Chinese culture to Japan

_____ **10.** Korea's name comes from this kingdom

a. haiku

b. Koryo

c. shogun

d. Lady Murasaki Shikibu

e. Prince Shotoku

READING STUDY GUIDE CONTINUED

Main Ideas

11. How was Japan affected by its closeness to China?

_____

_____

12. Why was Prince Shotoku an important leader in early Japan?

_____

_____

13. Why did Zen Buddhism become popular in Japan?

_____

_____

14. What are three unique forms of literature or drama created by the Japanese?

_____

_____

15. What led to a military government in Japan?

_____

_____

16. How were Korea and Southeast Asia hurt and helped by their nearness to China?

_____

_____

Thinking Critically

17. Making Inferences How did Japan's island location contribute to the development of unique forms of art and literature?

_____

_____

18. Making Generalizations What are three ways that ideas, practices, and beliefs of other cultures spread from China to other Asian countries?

_____

_____

CHAPTER 8

Lesson 1 The Development of Feudalism

BEFORE YOU READ

In this lesson, you will learn how Christianity spread and feudalism developed in Europe.

AS YOU READ

Use this chart to take notes on what role each group played in the feudal structure.

Lords	Vassals	Serfs

TERMS & NAMES

- **Middle Ages** a thousand year period (500–1450) in which small kingdoms dominated Europe
- **Charlemagne** king of the Franks who formed an empire in western Europe
- **monastery** place where religious followers practiced a life of prayer and worship
- **feudalism** a political system based on an agreement between lords and vassals
- **lord** a powerful noble who owned land
- **serf** person who lived and worked on the land belonging to a lord or vassal

Setting of Medieval Europe

(pages 291–293)

What changes occurred in Europe?

The Western Roman Empire fell in the late fifth century. This led to a period in Europe known as the **Middle Ages** (500–1450). This time is also known as the medieval period. During the Middle Ages, Europe became home to many small kingdoms.

Europe has a number of distinct geographic features. The European continent occupies the western part of the Eurasian land mass. This is the continuous stretch of land that includes Europe and Asia.

Europe borders the Atlantic Ocean on the west, the Arctic Ocean on the north, and the Mediterranean Sea on the south. In the east, the Ural Mountains separate Europe from Asia. Plains and farmland cover much of northern and western Europe. Europe has many rivers and lakes. Mild weather and steady rainfall encouraged farming throughout Europe.

Europe's geography played a key role in shaping the pattern of life during the Middle Ages. The favorable climate and many acres of good farmland enabled Europe's small kingdoms and estates to thrive

The political and social landscape of Europe changed greatly after the fall of Rome. Numerous Germanic groups controlled Europe. Unlike the Romans, Germanic people lived in small communities. They kept order through unwritten rules. They did not develop organized governments or trade systems.

Most schools disappeared during the Middle Ages. Eventually, few people could read or write Latin. Trade throughout Europe also declined. With less trade and commercial activity, most cities disappeared. Many people moved to the country. There, they made their living by farming.

CHAPTER 9

READING STUDY GUIDE CONTINUED

1. Why did many cities disappear after the fall of Rome?

_____

_____

Christianity Grows and Spreads

(pages 293–295)

How did Christianity grow?

One institution that survived the fall of Rome was the Christian Church. Many German rulers and their subjects converted to Christianity.

A powerful Germanic group called the Franks played a key role in strengthening Christianity in Europe. In the late 400s, a Frankish leader named Clovis defeated the last great Roman army in Gaul. By 507, his kingdom covered much of modern France. Around this time, Clovis converted to Christianity. In time, most of his subjects became Christians.

More than two centuries later, another powerful ruler led the Franks. His name was **Charlemagne.** He conquered new lands to the north and south. By 800, the Franks ruled much of western Europe. Charlemagne created a highly organized and well-run empire. He spread Christianity to the lands he conquered.

While strong rulers spread Christianity, so too did the work done in monasteries. **Monasteries** were places where religious followers practiced a life of prayer and worship. During the Middle Ages, monasteries arose across Europe. The religious followers who lived and worked in monasteries were known as monks. These people studied Christian works and wrote copies of the Bible. By doing so, they preserved and promoted Christian ideas and beliefs.

2. Which European leaders helped to spread Christianity?

_____

_____

Feudalism: A New Social Order

(pages 295–297)

What was feudalism?

Charlemagne died in 814. By the mid-800s, the Frankish kingdom became divided into three parts. This split caused the kingdom to grow weak. The decline of Frankish rule led to disorder across Europe.

Scandinavian pirates, called Vikings, and Muslims attacked coastal regions. A group known as the Magyars attacked towns throughout central Europe. Beginning in the mid-800s, Europe became a place of constant conflict and warfare.

With so much instability and violence, kings and nobles looked for a way to hold onto their power. To accomplish this, they developed a system known as **feudalism.** Feudalism was a political system based on an agreement between two groups of nobles— lords and vassals. A **lord** was a powerful noble who owned land. Lords gave pieces of their land to weaker nobles known as vassals. In return for the land, the vassal promised to protect the lord and his land. Many vassals were warriors known as knights.

Feudalism created a well-defined social structure throughout Europe. At the top of feudal society ruled the king. Next came wealthy landowners and high-ranking church members. Serving below them were knights. At the bottom of society were peasants. Most peasants were **serfs.** Serfs lived and worked on land that belonged to a lord or vassal. In return, the nobles granted them shelter and protection.

3. What agreement served as the basis of feudalism?

_____

_____

Lesson 2 Daily Life in Medieval Europe

BEFORE YOU READ

In this lesson, you will learn about daily life in medieval Europe.

AS YOU READ

Use this chart to take notes about the main differences between life on a manor and life in a town.

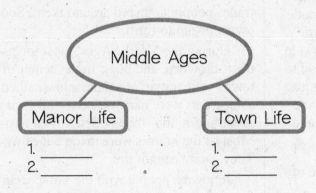

Middle Ages

Manor Life
1. _____
2. _____

Town Life
1. _____
2. _____

TERMS & NAMES
• **manor** the main part of a noble's land
• **knight** vassals, or lesser nobles, who fought for lords in return for land
• **chivalry** a code of honor for knights to follow
• **guild** a group of people with the same occupation

The Manor System

(pages 299–300)

What role did the manor play?

During the Middle Ages, strong central governments did not exist. Instead, Europe consisted of small kingdoms and lands held by high-ranking nobles. The main part of a noble's land was called a **manor.** The center of a manor was the house where the lord and his family lived. The manor house was often a castle. Surrounding the manor was the lord's estate. Much of the estate consisted of farmland.

The serfs were an important part of the lord's land. They lived and farmed on the land. This activity formed the economic basis of the manor system. The serfs were considered part of the manor's property. They remained on the land if a new lord bought it.

The land on the manor supplied the people living there with most of the things they needed. As a result, most economic activity took place on the manor. This activity included farming, woodworking, and wine making. Manors became worlds unto themselves. Few people ever left the property.

1. What made manors worlds unto themselves?

    _____

    _____

    _____

    _____

The Age of Chivalry

(pages 300–301)

What was chivalry?

During the Middle Ages, conflict often broke out between various lords. Many times, lords settled a quarrel by attacking each other. Lords relied on knights to do their fighting. **Knights** were vassals, or lesser nobles, who fought for lords in return for land.

Knights were more than just professional fighters. They were expected to live by a code of honor known as **chivalry.** According to this code, knights were expected to be loyal to their lord and brave in battle. They also had to show a strong religious faith and a willingness to defend Christianity. In addition, they were expected to protect women and the weak and fight against injustice.

2. What did the code of chivalry require of knights?

    _____

    _____

    _____

    _____

The Growth of Towns

(pages 301–302)

What was town life like?

By 1000, town life began to return to Europe. Over time, a number of lords became increasingly powerful. This brought greater peace and stability to many regions. As a result, merchants began to travel more freely. They also began to trade more goods. Wherever merchants settled, builders and trades people gathered around them. Soon towns began to form.

During the Middle Ages, most towns were dirty, crowded, and busy. In the center of most towns were a market square and a cathedral. The streets were narrow and usually not paved. After a rain, the streets often turned to mud. Most of the houses were made out of wood. They easily caught fire.

In towns, people with the same occupation formed groups called **guilds.** Many guilds were formed by trades people, such a goldsmiths and bakers. Guilds made rules that controlled the quantity and quality of production. The guilds also made sure that their members found employment.

3. What led to the growth of medieval towns?

    _____

    _____

    _____

    _____

Lesson 3 Feudalism in Europe and Japan

CHAPTER 9

BEFORE YOU READ

In this lesson, you will learn about the similarities and differences between the feudal societies in Europe and Japan.

AS YOU READ

Use this chart to compare the main political, social, and cultural characteristics of Japanese and European feudalism.

TERMS & NAMES

- **bushido** the samurai code of behavior
- **epic poem** a long poem that usually tells the story of warriors or heroes

	Political	Social	Culture
Europe			
Japan			

Similar Societies

(pages 307–308)

How was each society similar?

Japanese and European feudalism shared a number of similarities. In both lands, individual landowners gained power. This happened because strong central governments did not exist in either region. In Europe, strong landowners were called lords. In Japan, they were called daimyo.

Both lords and daimyo had many peasants working for them. Farming was the main economic activity on both European and Japanese estates. Both Japan and Europe relied on professionally trained soldiers for protection. In Europe, these soldiers were known as knights. They were known as samurai in Japan.

Both Japanese and European societies placed a high value military skills and loyalty. In Europe, knights had to follow a code of behavior known as chivalry. According to this code, knights were expected to be brave, loyal, and show kindness to the weak. The samurai code of behavior was known as **bushido.** This code promoted similar values to chivalry: courage, kindness, and loyalty to the daimyo, or lord.

1. What was one similarity between Japanese and European feudalism?

_____

_____

_____

CHAPTER 9

Cultural Differences

(pages 308–310)

How were the societies different?

The feudal systems of Japan and Europe differed in several significant ways. Knights and samurai practiced different religions. Knights were Christians. Samurai practiced ancient Shintoism. They also practiced a form of Buddhism known as Zen. Buddhism is based on the teaching of Buddha.

The literature that dominated each society also differed. Poetry called haiku became popular in feudal Japan. Haiku are short poems that follow a common pattern. In Europe, the epic poem became popular. An **epic poem** is a long poem that usually tells the story of warriors or heroes. Lyric poetry was also a significant part of European literature. These poems resembled songs. Most lyric poetry praised women and ideal love.

The status of women in each society also differed. In feudal Europe, the rights of women were limited. Medieval women, for example, had no say in whom they married. The woman's father often made this decision. In general, European women were expected to stay at home. Many were trained only in household chores, such as sewing, spinning, and farming.

Women in feudal Japanese society enjoyed more equal status with men. In samurai families, women were allowed to inherit part of the family's estate. Women also could join Buddhist convents. In addition, women were expected to live up to values of honor and courage. Often women were trained in martial arts. Gradually, the role of women became more restricted.

2. What religions did knights and samurai practice?

_____

_____

_____

Legacies of Feudalism

(pages 310–311)

What were the legacies of feudalism?

Both feudal Europe and Japan left lasting legacies. A legacy is something that is handed down from a previous generation or time. Aspects of feudal culture can be seen today in Japan and Europe. For example, Japanese weddings are usually based on a Shinto ceremony. In addition, haiku continues to be a popular form of poetry in Japan. Many Japanese continue to have a strong sense of loyalty to their family. This attitude stems from the old code of bushido.

The ideals of loyalty and honor also remain strong in Europe. This is especially true within the military. Another legacy of the European Middle Ages is surnames, or family names. Many European family names have medieval origins. During the Middle Ages, a person took a family name from his or her job. As a result, the family names Baker, Carpenter, and Cook are still common. In addition, many medieval structures, such as churches and castles, still stand in Europe. So do key institutions from this era, such as the Catholic Church.

3. What impact did the code of bushido have on Japan?

_____

_____

_____

Chapter 9 Feudal Europe

Glossary/After You Read

dominate to control or hold power over

devoted showing loyalty and affection; faithful

pirate a person who robs ships at sea

quarrel an argument or dispute

catapult a military device that throws missiles, such as rocks

courageous having the ability to face danger or difficulty bravely

strict following certain rules exactly

martial art a skill relating to self-defense or combat

Terms & Names

A. Circle the name or term that best completes each sentence.

1. Feudalism was a political system based on an agreement between _____ and vassals.

    serfs   lords   knights

2. The main part of a noble's land was called the _____.

    monastery   manor   town

3. Lesser nobles who fought for lords in return for land were called _____.

    serfs   dukes   knights

4. A _____ was a group made up of members of the same profession.

    guild   manor   daimyo

5. The samurai code of behavior was called _____.

    bushido   chivalry   Buddhism

B. Write the letter of the name or term that matches the description.

_____ **6.** king of the Franks who created a highly organized and well-run empire

_____ **7.** political system based on agreement between lords and vassals

_____ **8.** thousand-year period of many small kingdoms in Euope

_____ **9.** code of conduct that called for knights to show courage and kindness

_____ **10.** long poem usually about legendary heroes

_____ **11.** peasants who lived and worked on a lord's land

a. Charlemagne

b. chivalry

c. serfs

d. feudalism

e. epic poem

f. Middle Ages

Main Ideas

12. What helped Christianity to spread across Europe during the Middle Ages?

_____

_____

13. What were the various levels of feudal society?

_____

_____

14. What led to the growth of towns during the Middle Ages?

_____

_____

15. Did women enjoy a greater status in feudal Japan or Europe? Provide examples.

_____

_____

16. What legacies did feudalism leave in Europe?

_____

_____

Thinking Critically

17. Comparing and Contrasting How might a lord and serf differ in their views of feudalism?

_____

_____

_____

18. Drawing Conclusions What conclusions can you draw about European and Japanese culture based on their similarities and differences?

_____

_____

_____

Lesson 1 The Role of the Catholic Church

BEFORE YOU READ

In this section, you will read about the role of the Catholic Church in the rise of feudal societies in Europe.

AS YOU READ

Use this chart to summarize each of the main sections in Lesson 1.

Section	Summary
Power of the Church	
Conflict Between Monarchs and the Papacy	
The Church and Society	

TERMS & NAMES

- **Clergy** leaders of the Catholic Church such as cardinals, bishops, and priests
- **Pope Gregory VII** Eleventh century Pope who ended lay investiture, stopping King Henry IV from appointing clergy
- **religious order** a group of people who live together and follow the same religious rules
- **Francis of Assisi** Italian founder of a religious order of friars known as the Franciscans
- **Thomas Aquinas** Christian scholar who studied teachings of Aristotle in the mid 1200s

CHAPTER 10

Power of the Roman Catholic Church

(pages 321–323)

How did the Catholic Church become so powerful in medieval Europe?

At that time in Europe, there were no strong central governments or powerful rulers to unite people. Central authority was weak. Although at first the Catholic Church was small, it was very well organized. Church officials provided strong leadership at many levels from the Pope to the local priests. In time this helped the Church gain religious and political power and great wealth.

The **clergy** were the leaders of the Church. These men, especially the cardinals and bishops who filled the top positions in the Church, came from Europe's richest and most powerful families. They were well educated and could read and write Latin.

In time, the Church influenced political and legal affairs as well as religious issues.

Church officials took a key role in political life and assumed great legal power. Church leaders set up courts with power over those who broke church law. These courts decided cases and set punishments. The political power of the Church reached across Europe.

The great wealth of the Church strengthened its religious and legal powers. As the Church expanded, it acquired money and property. In time, the income from Church property made it richer than any single European country. Church leaders had more power than most European rulers.

1. What were three reasons why the Catholic Church became so powerful in medieval Europe?

_____

_____

_____

_____

READING STUDY GUIDE CONTINUED

Conflict Between Monarchs and the Papacy

(page 323)

What was the cause of conflict between Henry VII and Pope Gregory VII and what was the outcome?

For a long time, the Pope and other Church officials cooperated with European leaders. In the 11th century this changed. One cause of conflict was the struggle for power between the Church and the Holy Roman Empire.

The Holy Roman Empire was spread across most of present-day Germany and northern Italy. At this time, King Henry IV was its ruler. He built his political power by appointing key church officials such as bishops. Henry did so even though he was not a Church official. The king depended on these officials to help him hold onto political power. This was important to Henry because many nobles resented his power.

In 1075 **Pope Gregory VII** stopped King Henry IV from making these appointments. He ruled that only the Church could appoint religious officials. The Pope governed the Church from northern Italy. He feared that the Holy Roman Empire's control over northern Italy would threaten his own power.

King Henry fought back. He brought together the bishops who supported him. They declared that Pope Gregory had not been fairly elected. Gregory reacted by deciding to excommunicate, or banish, Henry from the Church.

After the Pope took this action, many nobles and church officials turned against Henry. Fearing he would lose his throne, Henry asked the Pope to forgive him. The Pope agreed, ending this conflict, but European political leaders and the Church would clash again over religious and political power.

2. Explain the cause and outcome of the conflict between Pope Gregory VII and King Henry IV.

_____

_____

The Church and Society

(pages 324–325)

What role did the Catholic Church play in education?

The most important way that the Church influenced education was through its religious orders. This is a group of people who live together and follow the same religious rules. These orders included monastic orders where monks and nuns lived. They were called monastic orders because their members lived in monasteries.

Friars were another type of **religious order.** They traveled from place to place preaching and spreading Church beliefs. Friars owned nothing and lived by begging. Italian friar **Francis of Assisi** founded an order of friars known as the Franciscans.

Monastic orders set up schools and libraries all over Europe, but by the 1100s there were not enough of these schools for all those who wanted to attend. Students came to cities where many learned teachers lived. They gathered to hear these teachers. In time, these gatherings grew into universities.

Church scholars also aided education by studying the writings of ancient Greek and Roman thinkers. In the mid 1200s, the Christian scholar **Thomas Aquinas** studied the works of the Greek philosopher Aristotle. He used his knowledge to argue that Church and government could get along as long as government laws followed the law of God. In time, such ideas led to new ways of thinking about government.

3. How did the Church help educate people in medieval Europe?

_____

_____

_____

CHAPTER 10

Lesson 2 The Crusades

BEFORE YOU READ

In the last section, you read about the power of the Catholic Church in Europe. In earlier lessons you read about the spread of Islam to parts of Southwest Asia, North Africa, and Europe. In this lesson you will learn about the effects of contact between Christians and Muslims.

AS YOU READ

Draw a timeline like the one below and use it fill in events as you read Lesson 2.

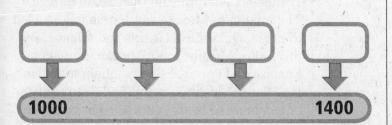

1000   1400

> **TERMS & NAMES**
>
> • **Seljuk Turk** Muslim group that took control of Palestine from the Muslim Abbasids in the mid 1200s
> • **Crusades** a series of religious wars by Christian armies to capture Palestine
> • **Saladin** Muslim political and military leader; united Egypt, Syria, Palestine, and other parts of Southwest Asia; recaptured Jerusalem
> • **Reconquista** the recapture of lands under Muslim control by Spain and Portugal
> • **Inquisition** court held by the Church to punish people, especially Jews and Muslims, whose religious beliefs differed from Church teachings

CHAPTER 10

Battle for Palestine

(pages 327–328)

Why did Christians want to conquer Palestine?
The **Crusades** took place from the 1000s to the 1300s. They were a series of religious wars by Christian armies to capture Palestine. Christian rulers from western Europe fought these wars to take Palestine from Muslim control. They wanted control of this area for religious and political reasons. European Christians thought of Palestine as a sacred site because of its connection to the life of Jesus. They called the area the Holy Land. This area is also sacred to Jews and Muslims.

Crusaders also went to war to help the Byzantine Empire. The Orthodox Christian rulers of the Byzantine Empire asked Catholic Christians in Europe for help in fighting the **Seljuk Turks.** At that time the Seljuk Turks

controlled Palestine. They threatened to invade the Byzantine Empire. Byzantine rulers turned to Catholic Europe for help in resisting this threat.

The First Crusade started in 1096. It began badly. European armies failed to take enough supplies. Tens of thousands died on the way. In Constantinople the Crusaders fought Muslim armies, winning control of a narrow strip of land along the Mediterranean. In 1099 they captured Jerusalem. Most of the Crusaders then returned to Europe. Those who stayed divided the land into four crusader states each ruled by a European noble.

1. Why did Christian leaders in Europe want to capture the Holy Land?

_____

_____

Muslims Return to Power

(pages 328–329)

How successful were the Muslim armies after the First Crusade?

The Second Crusade took place from 1147–1149. It began after Muslim Turks recaptured one of the Crusader states. This crusade ended in defeat for the Crusaders largely because the French and German armies failed to work together.

Until the late 1100s, other Crusader states remained under European control. Muslim armies failed to retake them because Muslims in Palestine and Egypt did not work together. By 1187, **Saladin,** a skilled military and political Muslim leader, had united Egypt, Syria, Palestine, and parts of Southwest Asia in a single state. Under his rule, Muslim armies took back much land lost during the First Crusade and recaptured Jerusalem.

News of Jerusalem's fall led Pope Gregory VIII to launch a Third Crusade (1189-1192). Crusaders failed to retake Jerusalem, but in 1192 the two sides agreed to stop fighting. Jerusalem remained under Muslim control, but Christians were allowed to visit the city's holy places.

2. What was Saladin's role in the Third Crusade?

_____

_____

Muslims Recapture Palestine

(pages 329–331)

How did the Crusades affect Europe?

Europeans led five more crusades. None succeeded. When the last one ended in 1270, Muslims had complete control of Palestine.

The Crusades helped and hurt Europe. The Crusades led to greater trade between Asia and Europe. Crusaders brought back Asian goods such as spices, cloth, and new foods like sugar and lemons. Crusaders also returned with large sums of money. Trade and the flow of money helped towns grow.

The Crusades weakened the feudal system. During the Crusades many feudal lords lost soldiers, money, and other resources. This weakened their power. Other national leaders like the king of France gained power.

The Crusades also caused new tensions between Christians, Jews, and Muslims. Crusaders murdered many Jews on their way to Palestine. Once there, they did the same to Muslims. Fear and hatred of Christians remained strong after the Crusades ended.

During the 700s, Muslims took control of the peninsula that includes Spain and Portugal. Under Muslim rule, Spain thrived. The mixing of Muslim and Jewish cultures led to great achievements in arts and science. By the 1000s, Muslim control began to weaken. Spanish and Portugal slowly fought to regain land under Muslim control. The **Reconquista,** or recapture of lands under Muslim control by Spain and Portugal, lasted almost 500 years. It ended in 1492. By then, Spanish rulers King Ferdinand and Queen Isabella had recaptured all lands under Muslim control.

Spain's rulers used their military and religious power to unite the Spanish people and end Muslim rule. Around 1480 they launched the **Inquisition.** This was a special court held by the Catholic Church to punish people, especially Jews and Muslims, who did not accept the Christian faith. Inquisition courts tortured and killed many Spanish Jews and Muslims. In 1492 Spanish armies drove out the last Muslim rulers. In that same year, Spain's ruler forced all Jews and Muslims to leave Spain.

3. How did the Crusades affect the economy and government of Europe and relations among religious groups?

_____

_____

CHAPTER 10 | LESSON 3 Plague and the Hundred Years' War

Lesson 3 Plague and the Hundred Years' War

BEFORE YOU READ

In the last section, you read how the Crusades lessened the power of feudal lords. In this lesson you will learn about events in Europe that weakened feudalism even more.

AS YOU READ

As you read Lesson 3, use a chart like the one below to list each main idea and details about it.

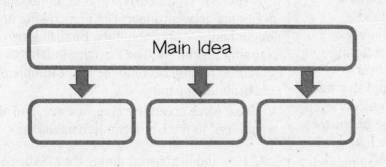

TERMS & NAMES

- **bubonic plague** a deadly disease caused by bacteria spread by fleas
- **Hundred Years' War** a series of wars between England and France that lasted from 1337 until 1453
- **Joan of Arc** a devout French Catholic who led the French to victory against rhe English at Orleans in 1429 and was later captured by allies of the English and killed
- **long bow** a bow about six feet tall that shoots 3-foot-long arrows that can pierce armor

The Plague

(pages 333–334)

How did the bubonic plague affect Europe in the 1300s?

In the 1300s the **bubonic plague** struck Europe. Before the end of the century, this deadly disease had killed about one-third of all Europeans and tens of millions of people worldwide.

The plague reached Europe in 1347. A trading ship brought the disease to Italy. From there it spread along European trade routes to France, Germany, and England.

A bacteria carried by fleas caused the plague. Infected fleas attached themselves to rats. From rats the fleas jumped to people. When fleas bit humans, people quickly became sick. About half of those who got the disease died, usually within days.

The plague caused a sharp drop in population in Europe. The loss of so many people upset daily life and made the world seem less orderly and safe. The drop in population also affected the economy. Europe had fewer workers. In many places workers were so scarce that laborers demanded and got much higher pay for their work.

1. What were two ways the plague affected Europe?

_____

_____

_____

_____

CHAPTER 10

READING STUDY GUIDE CONTINUED

The Hundred Years' War

(pages 335–336)

Who fought in the Hundred Years' War?

The **Hundred Years' War** lasted more than a hundred years from 1337 to 1453. France fought England. The war was not one long battle but a series of shorter conflicts. At times the fighting stopped because of peace agreements, the plague, and other events.

The war had many causes. The king of France wanted control of land in southern France claimed by the king of England. The French king made the English angry by arresting English merchants and interfering with England's trade with the continent. Fighting began in 1337 after the English king declared himself the true king of France. He based his claim to the French throne on the fact that he was nephew of the last French king.

At first the war went well for the England. The English won several major battles. By 1422 their armies had gained control of much of France. In 1429, however, the war turned in France's favor. Led by **Joan of Arc,** the French defeated the English in a battle at Orleans. Inspired by this victory, the French fought harder. By 1453, they had forced the English out of France, ending the war.

Before the Hundred Years' War, knights on horseback fought each other face-to-face with swords, axes, and lances. During the war, new weapons changed the way armies fought. With the **long bow** an archer could shoot large arrows at the enemy from great distances. French soldiers found new uses for the gunpowder invented by the Chinese. On the battlefield, they won many battles by firing artillery, large guns loaded with gunpowder.

2. What new weapons were used in the Hundred Years' War?

_____

_____

_____

Early Modern Europe Emerges

(pages 336–337)

How did social and political structures of Medieval Europe change?

Part of how historians define the end of the Middle Ages is the end of feudalism.

European towns grew and sought more stability. Strong monarchies could provide stability and towns became centers of support for the monarchies.

After the Hundred Years' War, monarchies in Europe grew stronger. The French king no longer had to worry about the English king claiming his throne. The French Monarchy would eventually become the best example of an absolute monarchy.

New ideas about learning, science, and art would lead to the European Renaissance.

3. How did life change during the Middle Ages?

_____

_____

_____

CHAPTER 10

Lesson 4 Changes in Government and Economics

BEFORE YOU READ

In the last section, you read about events that weakened feudalism in Europe. In this lesson, you will learn about changes in government and the economy.

AS YOU READ

As you read Lesson 4, use a chart like the one below to help you make generalizations. Start by listing details from different sections. Then write a general statement.

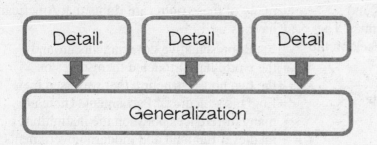

TERMS & NAMES

- **King John** the English king whose decision to raise taxes led to a revolt by nobles that forced him to recognize their rights in the Magna Carta
- **Magna Carta** 1215 document that listed the rights of English citizens and limited the power of the English monarch. Rights included trial by jury, no taxation without representation, protection of the law, and habeas corpus
- **parliament** representative legislative body
- **habeas corpus** protects people from being sent to prison without a trial

---

The English Government

(pages 341–342)

What were some of the new ideas about government in England?

English King Henry II created a common legal system by sending judges to every part of the country to hold court and settle conflicts. Over the years, the legal decisions made by these royal courts became known as common law. Common law rulings resulted in more equal treatment of English citizens under the law.

As the influence of royal courts grew, kings became more powerful. The growing power of the English king led to conflict between the king and the nobles. When **King John** raised taxes, his nobles revolted. They accused him of failing to recognize their rights. They

listed these rights in the document known as the **Magna Carta** and threatened to get rid of the king if he did not allow them these rights. Afraid of losing his throne, the king agreed.

1. How did new legal practices develop in England?

_____

_____

_____

_____

Representative Institutions

(page 343)

How did new ideas in politics change the government of England?

Another major step toward democratic government occurred in 1264. English nobles forced King Henry III to step down. They replaced him with a group of representatives later known as a **parliament.** This group included nobles, church officials, and townspeople. Although Henry's son Edward I retook the throne, he kept the parliament.

The parliament controlled taxes and Edward needed taxes to run the country. The parliament became an important check on the English ruler's power.

2. How did Parliament limit the power of the king?

_____

_____

_____

_____

Rise of Modern Democratic Thought

(pages 344–345)

What are some modern legal or political ideas that have their roots in medieval England?

Independent judiciaries, or courts, have developed around the world.

In time, all English people had the rights listed in the Magna Carta, not just nobles. This document also laid the foundation for the right of **habeas corpus.** This right protects people from being sent to prison without a trial. Today many of these rights are rights that Americans have as well.

Representative governments around the world have modeled themselves on the two house structure that was used by England's medieval Parliament. There are many differences between the institutions of medieval England and modern governments. Some modern governments can limit the power of the other parts of government. Changes like this happened over centuries.

3. Why are independent courts important to some modern governments?

_____

_____

_____

_____

Lesson 5 The Ottoman Empire

BEFORE YOU READ

In the other sections of this chapter, you read about European history. In this lesson, you will learn about the growth of the Ottoman Empire in Asia from the 1200s to the 1500s.

AS YOU READ

Use a chart like the one below to list each main idea and details about it.

Main Idea	Supporting Sentence
1	
2	
3	

TERMS & NAMES

- **Osman** a Muslim Turk who founded the Ottoman Empire in the early 1300s in Anatolia
- **divan** high court and council that advised the sultan of the Ottoman Empire
- **Suleyman I** ruler of the Ottoman Empire (1520-1566) known as Lawgiver because of his organization of certain laws into a legal code
- **janissary** elite Ottoman soldier

CHAPTER 10

An Emerging Power

(pages 351–352)

How did the Ottomans structure their empire?

After the Crusades, Mongols conquered the Seljuks. In time a new Turkish leader named **Osman** came to power. He founded the Ottoman Empire. Osman and the rulers who came after him expanded the empire by buying land, forming alliances, and conquering other groups. The sultan was the head of the Ottoman government. Below him was the **divan.** This was the high court and council that advised the sultan. The grand vizier was the head of the divan and the sultan's main representative.

Military leaders, religious leaders, and owners of large estates belonged to the highest class in Ottoman society. They were the ruling class. Slaves also filled key positions in government.

Suleyman I came to power in 1520. He was called "the Lawgiver" by his people because of his organizations of the Ottoman legal code.

1. Why was the Ottoman Empire a threat to Europe?

_____

_____

_____

_____

The Empire Expands

(page 352)

What regions did the Ottomans expand into?

Led by Suleyman, the Ottomans marched into Hungary and Austria, hoping to gain control of central Europe. They went almost to Vienna, Austria. There Ottoman expansion ended. Suleyman had to withdraw his forces after he ran out of supplies.

Under Suleyman, the Ottoman Empire covered more territory than at any other time. They controlled much of southwest Asia, northern Africa, and parts of southeastern Europe.

The Ottomans also brought an end to the Byzantine Empire. In 1453, they captured Constantinople and changed its named to Istanbul and made it their capitol. The Ottomans allied with France and tried to defeat the German Hapsburgs, but ultimately had to retreat from Vienna, Austria.

2. How far did the Ottomans expand into Europe?

_____

_____

_____

_____

Life in the Ottoman Empire

(pages 353–354)

What was the Ottoman policy toward Christians?

They gave Christians and Jews great freedom. They allowed Christians and Jews freedom of worship. Both groups were able to establish their own communities, called millets. As long as millets remained loyal and paid their taxes, they could practice their religion, follow their own religious laws and customs, speak their own languages, and govern themselves.

The Ottomans developed a system of slave soldiers that was the elite of the Ottoman army. They were called **janissaries.** They had gunpowder weapons and helped expand the empire.

The situation of women under the Ottomans depended on their social class and where they lived. Islamic law gave women the right to divorce and to inherit property. In cities, women could work in shops and in the country they worked in the fields with the men. Women of the sultan's court received an education, but did not have many freedoms.

The sultans' power slowly declined while powerful European monarchies were on the rise.

3. How were women treated in the Ottoman Empire?

_____

_____

_____

_____

CHAPTER 10

Chapter 10 Medieval Europe and the Ottoman Empire

Glossary/After You Read

clergy leaders of the Catholic Church such as cardinals, bishops, and priests

Francis of Assisi Italian founder of a religious order of friars known as the Franciscans

Crusades a series of religious wars by Christian armies to capture Palestine

Reconquista the recapture of lands under Muslim control by Spain and Portugal

Inquisition court held by the Roman Catholic Church

bubonic plague a deadly disease caused by bacteria spread by fleas

Magna Carta 1215 document that listed the rights of English citizens and limited the power of the English monarch. Rights included trial by jury, no taxation without representation, protection of the law, and habeas corpus

parliament representative legislative body

Suleyman I ruler of the Ottoman Empire (1520-1566) known as Lawgiver because of his organization of certain laws into a legal code

Terms & Names

A. If the statement is true, write "true" on the line. If it is false, change the underlined word or words to make it true.

_____ **1.** A <u>clergy</u> is a group of people who live together and follow the same religious rules.

_____ **2.** The <u>Reconquista</u> were a series of wars fought by Christian powers to take Palestine from Muslim control.

_____ **3.** The <u>Hundred Years' War</u> was a series of wars between France and England between 1337 and 1453.

_____ **4.** The <u>Magna Carta</u> listed the rights of English nobles such as trial by jury.

_____ **5.** The <u>Reconquista</u> was the capture of Palestine.

B. Write the letter of the name or term that matches the description.

_____ **6.** English ruler who raised taxes causing nobles to revolt.

_____ **7.** French peasant who led France to victory in battle against the English

_____ **8.** Muslim political leader during the Crusades

_____ **9.** The religious leader who ruled that only the Church could appoint religious officials and banned Henry IV from the Church.

_____ **10.** Greatest leader of the Ottoman Empire, known as "The Lawgiver"

a. Gregory VII

b. Saladin

c. Joan of Arc

d. King John

e. Suleyman

READING STUDY GUIDE CONTINUED

Main Ideas

11. What was the main reason for conflict between European monarchs and popes?

_____

_____

12. How did the Crusades affect Europe?

_____

_____

13. Why were the 1300s a century of crisis?

_____

_____

_____

14. How did European governments change as a result of the Hundred Years' War?

_____

_____

15. How did conflict between English kings and nobles in the 1200s change government?

_____

_____

16. Why was the Ottoman Empire an important place for Muslim scholars and religious leaders?

_____

_____

Thinking Critically

17. Forming and Supporting Opinions Why do you think the Magna Carta was such an important step toward democratic government in England?

_____

_____

18. Forming and Supporting Opinions Why do you think Ottoman rulers allowed different religions to live in peace?

_____

_____

Lesson 1 Geography and Agriculture in Mesoamerica

BEFORE YOU READ

In this lesson, you will learn about the geography of Mesoamerica and how this geography shaped the lives of Mesoamericans.

AS YOU READ

Use this chart to take notes about the geography of Mesoamerica. Answering the question at the end of each section will help you fill in the chart.

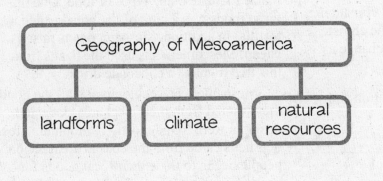

TERMS & NAMES

- **Mesoamerica** a region that lies between the United States and South America
- **Yucatán Peninsula** a lowland region in southeast Mexico that stretches into, and divides, the Caribbean Sea and the Gulf of Mexico
- **elevation** the height of land above sea level
- **slash-and-burn agriculture** a method of farming that involves clearing land by cutting trees, burning the trees, using the ashes to fertilize the land, and then planting crops on the land
- **maize** a type of corn
- **cacao** a type of tree that produces beans used to make chocolate

Landforms of Mesoamerica

(pages 367–368)

What landforms are found in Mesoamerica?

Mesoamerica includes the southern part of Mexico and much of Central America.

Mountains run down the center of Mesoamerica. In the north, the mountain range divides into two. A region called the Mexican Plateau separates these two highland areas. Coastal plains wind along the Pacific Ocean, the Caribbean Sea, and the Gulf of Mexico. Here and there, the plains widen into broad lowlands. One such area is the **Yucatán Peninsula,** which stretches into, and divides, the Caribbean Sea and the Gulf of Mexico.

Volcanoes have changed the landscape of Mesoamerica. When a volcano erupts, it spits out streams of lava, or melted rock. It also releases clouds of ash. In time, the lava and ash build up. Eventually, they form huge cone-like mountains. More than a dozen of these Mesoamerican volcanic mountains are still active. That means they can erupt at any time. Most have been dormant, or inactive, for hundreds of years.

1. What is the landscape like in Mesoamerica?

_____

_____

Climate and Vegetation

(page 368)

How do climates vary in Mesoamerica?

Much of Mesoamerica lies in the Tropics. Generally, the climates there are hot and wet. The heat and moisture give rise to rain forests. Many different kinds of trees and plants grow there. Less rain falls in lowland areas. As a result, the lowlands are covered with grasslands.

Northern Mesoamerica has a hot, dry climate. Much of this area is covered with grasslands. Some parts of the north get so little rain that they are considered a desert.

Elevation, or the height of the land above sea level, has a strong influence on climate in Mesoamerica. As elevation rises, the climate grows cooler. Growing conditions change as climate changes.

2. What is the link between elevation and climate?

_____

_____

Geography Shapes Mesoamerican Life

(pages 369–371)

How has geographic diversity affected the natural resources and crops found in Mesoamerica?

The highlands of Mesoamerica supplied jade and obsidian. Obsidian is a black volcanic glass. Mesoamericans made small carvings from jade. They made sharp weapons from obsidian. Coastal regions provided seashells and shark's teeth. Mesoamericans used these for jewelry.

Mesoamericans also made use of the animals found in the region. They prized the colorful feathers of a bird called the quetzal. The quetzal was sacred to many Mesoamericans. They often used the feathers from these birds to decorate their clothing.

Mesoamericans farmed all kinds of land. Floodplains of rivers and the slopes of volcanic mountains had fertile soil. As a result, these lands were good for growing crops. Other areas, such as rain forests, were not good for growing crops. To work these lands, Mesoamericans used a method called **slash-and-burn agriculture.** Farmers cleared the land by cutting down trees. Then they burned the fallen trees. Next, they used the ashes to fertilize the soil. Finally, they planted crops on the cleared land. After a few years, they left this land and moved to another part of the rain forest.

Mesoamericans grew a variety of crops, including **maize**—a type of corn. They also grew beans, peppers, and squash. They used maize to make many types of food. One of these foods was a kind of flat bread called a tortilla. In addition, Mesoamericans raised **cacao.** Mesoamericans used the beans from this tree to make a chocolate drink.

Mesoamericans could not get all the goods they wanted from their local area. Jade and obsidian were found mostly in mountain areas. Seashells came from the coastal areas. Soon people began to trade their local goods for goods found in other regions.

Mesoamericans traded goods over great distances by water and overland. Using dugout canoes, they traveled the rivers in the region. They also traveled along the Pacific, Caribbean, and Gulf coasts. The Mesoamericans did not develop the wheel. Also there were no horses or oxen to use as pack animals. Even so, the Mesoamericans still carried on an overland trade. They did this by carrying the goods on their backs.

More than goods traveled along the trade routes. Traders also carried knowledge with them. This knowledge spread all over the region. This sharing of ideas helped to create a common culture throughout Mesoamerica.

3. How did the geography of Mesoamerica encourage trade?

_____

_____

CHAPTER 11

Lesson 2 The Olmec Civilization

BEFORE YOU READ

In this lesson, you will learn about the "mother culture" of Mesoamerica, the Olmec civilization.

AS YOU READ

Use this chart to take notes about major features of the Olmec civilization. Answering the question at the end of each section will help you fill in the chart.

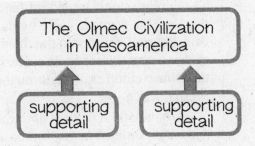

TERMS & NAMES

- **Olmec** a group of people who lived along the Gulf coast in southern Mexico about 3,000 years ago
- **alluvial soil** soil deposited by flowing water
- **elite** the upper class of a society
- **glyph** picture that represents a word, syllable, or sound
- **mother culture** a way of life that strongly influences later cultures

An Early American Civilization

(pages 373–374)

Why were the Olmec able to develop one of the earliest civilizations in the Americas?

About 3,000 years ago, the **Olmec** lived in what is now southern Mexico. At first, they settled along rivers near the Gulf Coast. They got much of their food from fishing. Later, the Olmec began to farm. This activity helped them to develop the first major civilization in Mesoamerica.

The Olmec realized that the flat lands near rivers were good for growing crops. The **alluvial soil**—soil deposited by running water—that covered these lands was very fertile. In time, farmers began to do very well in this region. As a result, the food supply increased. It also became very steady. With a steady food supply, the Olmec population grew.

Also, the steady food supply meant that not everyone had to farm. This allowed some people to focus on other tasks. Some became potters or weavers. Others became priests or teachers.

As the Olmec population grew, so too did their farming villages. Some of these villages developed into cities. By 1150 B.C., the Olmec had built a large city that is now called San Lorenzo. The center of the city contained raised mounds and large stone monuments. The monuments were used for religious ceremonies. San Lorenzo also had areas used for trade. In addition, the city had housing areas, where Olmec priests and rulers lived.

Another huge Olmec city began to grow around 900 B.C. This city is now called La Venta. Eventually, it replaced San Lorenzo as the center of the Olmec civilization. Like San Lorenzo, La Venta served as a religious and trade center.

1. What impact did an increased and more reliable food supply have on the Olmec?

_____

_____

CHAPTER 11

Olmec Culture

(pages 374–376)

What kind of culture did the Olmec develop?

Most Olmec were farmers and fishers. They lived in villages near rivers. The Olmec grew maize, beans, squash, and peppers. They caught fish and turtle and hunted deer

Most of the Olmec who lived in cities were from the **elite,** an upper class of priests and nobles who ruled Olmec society. These people lived in large houses made of stone. They wore jewelry and fancy clothes. Some commoners also lived in the cities. Their houses were smaller and made of wood or mud. And their clothes were very plain. They mostly were laborers and craftworkers.

The Olmec played a ball game that was very popular with their people. The game was played in huge ball courts. The Olmec may have invented the game.

San Lorenzo and other Olmec cities contained several huge, stone heads. Each head has a flat face, thick lips, and staring eyes. The purpose of these heads remains unknown. They may be monuments to Olmec rulers. Or they could be famous ball game players. The Olmec made the heads out of basalt, a kind of volcanic rock.

The Olmec also made small sculptures out of jade. Other Olmec art included pottery and cave paintings. The Olmec used an early form of **glyph** writing. Glyphs are pictures that represent words, syllables, or sounds. They used this writing to record events, dates, and to tell stories. The Olmec also developed a very accurate calendar.

The Olmec worshiped several gods. The chief god was the jaguar. They probably believed that the jaguar god brought rain. The Olmec also worshiped a fire god and a corn god. As you read earlier, the Olmec built large mounds in the centers of their cities. Later, the Olmec replaced these mounds with pyramids. The Olmec probably used the pyramids as religious centers.

2. How was Olmec society organized?

_____

_____

_____

The Olmec Legacy

(pages 376–377)

Why did Olmec culture have a lasting influence in Mesoamerica?

Most Olmec cities served as trade centers. The Olmec mainly traded for fancy items that the elite wanted. These items included valuable stones and iron ore. Ideas also were exchanged at Olmec trade centers. As a result, the Olmec culture spread throughout much of Mesoamerica.

Around 500 B.C., the Olmec began to leave their cities. The reason for this remains unclear. By 400 B.C., the Olmec civilization had largely disappeared. Even so, it had a huge impact on Mesoamerica.

Many historians consider the Olmec civilization the mother culture of Mesoamerica. A **mother culture** is a way of life that strongly influences later cultures. Olmec culture and customs shaped the Mesoamerican cultures that followed. These cultures included the Zapotec, the people of Teotihuacán, the Aztec, and especially the Maya.

3. Why is Olmec civilization considered a mother culture?

_____

_____

_____

CHAPTER 11

Lesson 3 The Mayan Civilization

BEFORE YOU READ

In this lesson, you will learn about the Maya, one of the most highly developed civilizations in Mesoamerica.

AS YOU READ

Use this chart to help you learn about the Maya. Enter in the chart several questions about the Mayan civilization that you would like answered. As you read this lesson, record in the chart any answers that you find.

Questions	Answers
Where was the Myan civilization located?	

TERMS & NAMES

- **Maya** groups of Mesoamerican peoples who speak various forms of the Mayan language
- **stele** a large stone monument that was often carved with symbols or glyphs
- **Pacal II** king of the Mayan city of Tikal
- **codex** a type of book made out of bark paper that is screen-folded

Birth of a Civilization

(page 380)

Where did Mayan civilization arise?

Today, the **Maya** live in southern Mexico, Guatemala, and northern Belize. Their culture can be traced as far back as 2000 B.C.

Around 1500 B.C., the Maya began to establish villages. These villages were located in the highlands and lowlands of Mesoamerica. The highlands contained many minerals. In general, the highlands had a dry, cool climate.

The lowlands on the Yucatán Peninsula had a hot, dry climate. Hot, humid rain forests covered the lowlands further to the south. This area had fertile soil.

Farming did very well in the Mayan lowlands. Because of this, the Maya were able to grow much food. With more food, the Maya became healthier. As a result, their population grew. In time, some Mayan farming villages grew into great cities.

1. Where did the Maya establish villages?

_____

_____

Mayan Life

(pages 382–384)

Into what social classes was Mayan society divided?

The Maya produced more than enough food. Because of this, some people could focus on tasks other than farming. Some became craftworkers. Other became priests or teachers. This division of labor resulted in the growth of a class system.

Mayan society was made up of four social classes. These were the ruling class, the nobility, peasants, and slaves.

The ruling class was made up of kings and their families. These rulers also performed the religious duties of priests. A king governed each Mayan city. The nobility probably included scholars and merchants. They were educated and wealthy. Peasants included farmers and laborers. Most of the Maya were peasants. Slaves were mostly criminals and people captured in war.

Mayan farmers lived in small villages near the big cities. They lived in simple homes. Mayan farmers grew maize, beans, chili peppers, and cacao. Maize was the most important crop. The Maya believed they had been created out of maize.

Mayan nobles led very different lives from the peasants. They wore fancy clothes and much jewelry. Nobles lived in houses built of stone. They also ate much better than peasants.

The Maya worshiped more than 160 gods and goddesses. The main god was called ItzamNá. The Maya believed this god created the world. To get help from the gods, the Maya often fasted, prayed, and offered sacrifices. Most of these sacrifices were animals. The Maya also offered their own blood as a sacrifice. Occasionally, the Maya made human sacrifices. The Maya expected their rulers to communicate with the gods on their behalf.

The Maya had many religious festivals and ceremonies. One important ceremony was a ball game. It was performed in a large ball court. The ball game may have been played to honor great Mayan heroes. Or it was played to reenact important events from Mayan history. Sometimes it was just a sporting competition.

2. What were the four classes that made up Mayan society?

_____

_____

Glory and Decline
(pages 384–386)

What developments did the Maya achieve during their Classical period?

The Maya reached their peak roughly during the years between A.D. 250 and 900.

The Maya built more than 40 cities. Each Mayan city contained pyramids with temples on top of them. Many of them also had **steles.** The Maya carved glyphs on these large stone monuments. The glyphs represented important dates and great events.

A king governed each Mayan city and the surrounding areas. One of the greatest Mayan kings was **Pacal II,** who ruled the city of Tikal. Sometimes cities fought each other. The winners gained political and economic advantages. The Maya developed a complex writing system. This system used glyphs. The Maya carved glyphs on buildings. They also wrote them on bark paper. This paper was screen-folded to form a type of book called a **codex.** Few of these books still exist. The most famous is the *Popol Vuh.* It tells the Mayan story of the creation.

The Maya developed a mathematical system based on the number 20. Also, the Maya were one of the first people to use zero. By using their math system, the Maya made great advances in astronomy. The Maya also produced a very accurate calendar system.

Beginning in the 800s, the Maya began to leave their cities in the southern lowlands. At the same time, their population declined sharply. The reasons for these events remain a mystery. By the 1400s, the Maya had left all their cities.

3. What advances did the Maya achieve in record keeping?

_____

_____

Chapter 11 Early Mesoamerican Civilizations

Glossary/After You Read

spine something that resembles a backbone

crater a hollow area shaped like a bowl at the mouth of a volcano

commoner a person who is not of noble birth; a common person

spectator a person who watches, rather than takes part in, an event

criminal a person who has broken the law

mural painting applied to walls or ceilings

fast go purposefully without all or certain foods

Terms & Names

A. Circle the name or term that best completes each sentence.

1. The height of land above sea level is called _____.

   humidity   elevation   atmosphere

2. A type of tree that produces beans used to make chocolate is called a _____ tree.

   palm   cacao   maize

3. Soil deposited by flowing water is called _____.

   alluvial   glyph   elite

4. Pictures that represent words, syllables, or sounds are called _____.

   codices   icons   glyphs

5. Large stone monuments that are often carved with symbols are called _____.

   plazas   steles   tablets

B. Write the letter of the name or term that matches the description.

_____ 6. a way of life that strongly influences later cultures

_____ 7. a region that lies between the United States and South America and includes southern Mexico and much of Central America

_____ 8. a group of people in southern Mexico who carved large heads out of basalt

_____ 9. scholars and merchants in Mayan society

_____ 10. a lowland region in southeast Mexico between that juts into the Caribbean Sea and the Gulf of Mexico

_____ 11. a ceremony that honored great Mayan heroes or re-enacted past events

a. Mesoamerica

b. nobility

c. Olmec

d. Yucatán Peninsula

e. mother culture

f. ball game

Main Ideas

12. What is slash-and-burn agriculture?

_____

_____

13. How are volcanic mountains formed?

_____

_____

14. What social classes was Olmec society divided into? Describe each class.

_____

_____

_____

15. Why did Mayan cities fight each other?

_____

_____

16. What resources did the Maya get from the highlands and lowlands of Mesoamerica?

_____

_____

Thinking Critically

17. Forming and Supporting Opinions Why do you think the Olmec civilization declined? Give reasons to support your answer.

_____

_____

_____

18. Comparing and Contrasting How were the Mayan ruling class and nobility similar and different?

_____

_____

_____

CHAPTER 11

CHAPTER 12 | LESSON 1 The Aztecs

Lesson 1 The Aztecs

BEFORE YOU READ

In Chapter 7, you read about early civilizations in Mesoamerica. In this lesson, you will read about the rise and fall of the greatest empire in that region, the Aztec empire.

AS YOU READ

Use a "chain of events" diagram like the one below. Show the sequence of events in the rise and fall of the Aztec Empire.

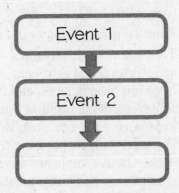

Event 1

Event 2

TERMS & NAMES

• **Tenochtitlán** Capital city built by the Aztecs on an island in Lake Texcoco, site of Mexico City today

• **Montezuma II** Aztec emperor who came to power in 1502, captured by Spanish troops and killed in fighting between the Spanish and Aztecs

• **Hernán Cortés** leader of Spanish troops who conquered Aztec empire

Aztecs Settle in Central Mexico

(pages 397–398)

How did the Aztecs adapt to the Valley of Mexico?

The Aztecs settled in the Valley of Mexico in the late 1200s. No major power controlled the region when they arrived. The area had some small city-states ruled by various peoples. These groups held the most fertile land. The Aztecs claimed the rest.

A legend says that the Aztec sun and war god told the Aztecs they should settle where they saw an eagle sitting on a cactus. In 1325, they found such a place near a large lake. There they built the city of **Tenochtitlán.** This city became their capital.

The lands around Tenochtitlán were not well suited to farming. The land was swampy. High mountains surrounded it. There was little flat land for farming and no wood or stone nearby for building. The Aztecs adapted by building *chinampas,* or floating gardens, on the lake. They grew corn, squash, and other

crops on the *chinampas.* With enough food, the population of Technoctitlán increased and spread out around the lake. Trade was important to the Aztec economy. The Aztecs traded for goods they could not get locally.

Over time, the Aztec empire grew very large. It expanded by making alliances with some city-states and by conquering others. The Aztecs demanded *tribute,* or a forced payment, from the peoples they conquered. Tribute was usually in corn, gold, and jade.

1. How did the Aztecs build a powerful empire?

_____

_____

Aztec Society and Beliefs

(pages 399–400)

How was Aztec society organized?

Aztec society was divided into three highly structured groups, or classes. These were

CHAPTER 12

nobles, the intermediate class, and commoners. The emperor was at the top of Aztec society. He belonged to the noble class. The nobles were the smallest but most powerful class. They owned large estates and ran the government and military. Priests also belonged to this class.

The intermediate class was made up of merchants and highly skilled artisans. Most people were commoners. They made up the largest and lowest class. Some commoners were landowning farmers, fishers, craftworkers, and soldiers. Landless workers and slaves were below them.

The Aztecs lived in family groups in large communities. Most men farmed their own or a noble's lands. Women cooked, tended children, and did chores.

Religion was a key part of daily life. The Aztecs worshipped about 1000 agricultural gods. Priests in the temples set the times for services and conducted them. The most important ceremonies were held to ask the gods for a good harvest. At these services, humans were sacrificed to the gods. They were usually prisoners of war. War was a religious duty for Aztec warriors. It provided more land and people for the empire and victims for human sacrifice.

As the empire grew, so did the need for farmland. Emperors and nobles also wanted more tribute. The Aztecs constantly fought and conquered other groups to meet these needs.

In 1502, an emperor named **Montezuma II** came to power. He demanded more tribute and victims for sacrifice. The harsh treatment by the Aztecs and the demand for more tribute angered many conquered peoples. Some rebelled. This weakened Aztec power.

In 1519, Spanish troops under **Hernán Cortés** invaded the Valley of Mexico. They easily captured Montezuma and took control of the empire. The Spanish were victorious mainly because thousands of rebels helped them conquer Tenochtitlán. They also won because they had superior weapons, such as

muskets, cannon, body armor, and horses. Diseases brought by the Europeans also weakened the Aztecs.

2. What were three reasons why the Spanish defeated the Aztecs?

_____

_____

The Cultural Legacy of the Aztecs

(pages 401–402)

What cultural advances did the Aztec make?

The Aztecs made advances in the arts, architecture, and astronomy. They built large temples, palaces, and city walls. Aztec achievements in building can still be seen in Mexico City. The Spanish built Mexico City over Tenochtitlán, but the remains of the Aztec Great Temple are there. From other remains, we know that artists made gold beads, pottery, stone urns, feather headdresses, stone sculpture, and jewelry.

The Aztecs had a spoken language, but wrote using a picture or symbol, called a glyph, to represent a word or idea. The Aztecs collected their writings in a book of glyphs called a codex. Each codex gives details of Aztec life. Scholars have learned about Aztec life from these codices, or illustrated books.

Farming was important to the Aztecs, and they needed to know the best time to plant and harvest. So, the Aztecs studied the sun, moon, stars, and planets. They used this information to make two calendars. They had a farming calendar for planting and harvesting and a religious calendar for planning religious ceremonies.

3. What was the Aztecs' cultural legacy?

_____

_____

CHAPTER 12

Lesson 2 The Inca

BEFORE YOU READ

In the last lesson, you read about the Aztecs who built the greatest empire in Meso-America. In this lesson, you will read about the Inca who created a great empire in South America.

AS YOU READ

Use a graphic like the one below to identify the methods the Inca used to build their vast empire.

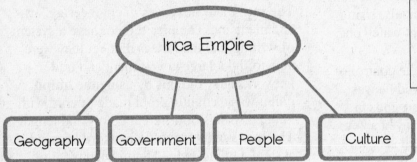

TERMS & NAMES
• **Pachacuti** considered the greatest Inca emperor
• *chasqui* Incan runners who provided a communication system by carrying messages throughout the empire
• **Francisco Pizarro** Spanish explorer and conqueror of the Inca Empire
• **quipu** Incan counting tool made of a cord with knotted strings

Geography of a Mountain Empire

(pages 408–411)

How did the Inca adapt their way of life to living in high mountains?

The Inca lived in the high and rugged Andes Mountains in what is now Peru. In the 1200s, they settled in a fertile mountain valley high above sea level. There they built their capital city Cuzco.

Over time, the Inca Empire slowly expanded. In 1438, **Pachacuti** became the ninth Inca ruler. Under Pachacuti, the Inca conquered all of Peru and moved into surrounding lands. His son and grandson conquered additional territory during their rules. By 1500, the Inca Empire stretched 2,500 miles along the west coast of South America.

The high mountains, rough terrain, and varied people made governing the empire hard. The Inca tried to unite conquered peoples by dividing them into family groups. Incan leaders also united them by requiring them to learn to speak the Inca language and worship Incan gods.

Farming was difficult in the Andes because the land was high and steep. Incan farmers cut flat steps or terraces into steep mountainsides to create more farmland. They built irrigation systems to bring water to their fields. They also raised llamas and alpacas for meat and wool in high areas too cold and dry for crops.

The government built a vast network of roads to meet the challenge of communication. Runners called *chasquis* carried messages all over the empire on these roads. Each year the Incan government required its subjects to spend time building and repairing the roads.

1. Why was the network of roads important to the success of the Inca Empire?

_____

_____

CHAPTER 12

Incan Society and Beliefs

(pages 412–413)

How did Incan society develop?

The Incan ruler, or emperor, was at the top of Incan society. Incan society had two main groups—nobles and commoners. Nobles ran the army and had a rich life style. Most commoners were farmers or fishers. They provided food for nobles, priests, and everyone else in Incan society. Some were artisans.

The emperor was a very powerful ruler. He kept tight control of nearly all aspects of daily life through his government officials. Using local chiefs, the government kept watch on even the smallest villages.

The Incan people accepted the control of the emperor because they believed he was divine. The Inca worshipped their gods in temples run by priests. Priests played a key role in Incan life. They performed special ceremonies when the emperor needed to make a major decision and made animal sacrifices for a good harvest.

The Incan army was the most powerful military force in the Andes. Most of its nearly 200,000 soldiers were commoners. They were mainly Incan farmers or people from conquered territories. Officers were always Incan nobles.

In 1528, a bitter civil war weakened the empire. The conflict took place between followers of a leader named Atahualpa and followers of his brother. Thousands died as the two sides fought for control of the empire. Atahualpa's forces won.

The civil war was just ending when Spanish explorer **Francisco Pizarro** and his troops arrived on the coast in 1532. Pizarro asked to meet with Atahualpa. The emperor agreed. When he arrived, the Spanish captured and later killed him. The Inca Empire began to fall apart after his death. The Spanish controlled most Inca lands by 1535.

Thousands of Inca died from diseases brought by the Europeans over the next decades. Many others were captured and enslaved by the Spanish. The Inca Empire ended when the last Inca ruler was defeated in 1572.

2. What caused the fall of the Inca Empire?

_____

_____

The Cultural Legacy of the Inca

(pages 414–415)

What advances did the Inca make in science, technology, and the arts?

The Inca made advances in engineering, art, and medicine. The Inca did not have a system of writing like the Aztecs did. Yet they were able to run a large government and trade network. They did this by using the **quipu.** A quipu was a counting tool made of cord with knotted strings of different colors and lengths. The Inca used this tool as a record keeping system. Quipus helped them keep track of trade goods, military troops, and populations in the territories. Another type of quipu helped the Inca recall their history. Symbols tied to strings stood for ideas and events.

The Inca were gifted builders. They created a vast network of roads, tunnels, and bridges. The Inca were also skilled engineers. They built forts, palaces, and temples using huge stone blocks. Some still stand. Incan craftspeople made jewelry out of precious metals such as gold. Weavers made beautiful cloth from alpaca wool. These crafts are still practiced today.

The Inca also made medical advances. They studied sick people and learned about local plants. They used this knowledge to make medicines from plants. Inca surgeons even did an early type of brain surgery.

3. What were the cultural contributions of the Inca?

_____

_____

CHAPTER 12

Chapter 12 Later American Civilizations

Glossary/After You Read

basin a bowl-shaped depression in the surface of the land

aggressive assertive, bold, or combative

tended looked after; taken care of

perched sat upon or rested on

Terms & Names

A. If the statement is true, write "true" on the line. If it is false, change the underlined word or words to make it true.

_____ **1.** <u>Montezuma II</u> was the ruler of the Aztec Empire when the Aztecs first arrived in the Valley of Mexico.

_____ **2.** The Aztec built <u>Tenochtitlán</u> high in the Andes Mountains in a river valley.

_____ **3.** <u>Pachacuti</u> was the Inca ruler who expanded the Inca Empire.

_____ **4.** <u>Francisco Pizarro</u> led the Spanish in their conquest of the Aztec Empire.

_____ **5.** The <u>quipu</u> helped the Inca run the government by keeping track of key information like numbers of trade goods or troops.

B. Write the letter of the name or term that matches the description.

_____ **6.** Ninth and greatest Inca ruler   **a.** quipu

_____ **7.** Inca counting tool   **b.** Pachacuti

_____ **8.** Aztec capital city   **c.** *chasqui*

_____ **9.** Inca runners   **d.** Tenochtitlan

_____ **10.** Spanish conqueror of the Aztec Empire   **e.** Hernan Cortes

READING STUDY GUIDE CONTINUED

Main Ideas

11. How did the Aztec adapt their way of farming to the geography of the Valley of Mexico?

_____

_____

12. What classes made up Aztec society and which one had the most power?

_____

_____

13. What advances did the Aztecs make in architecture and astronomy?

_____

_____

14. How did the Inca adapt their way of life to the mountainous terrain?

_____

_____

15. What religious belief helped the Inca emperor control the people of the empire?

_____

_____

16. What was unique about the Inca method of recordkeeping?

_____

_____

Thinking Critically

17. Making Inferences Why did the Aztecs make advances in astronomy?

_____

_____

18. Comparing and Contrasting In what ways were the fall of the Inca and Aztec empires alike?

_____

_____

Lesson 1 Origins of the Renaissance

BEFORE YOU READ

In this lesson, you will learn about the decline of feudalism and the origins of the Renaissance.

AS YOU READ

Use this chart to take notes about the origins of the Renaissance. Answering the question at the end of each section will help you fill in the chart.

TERMS & NAMES

- **Silk Roads** ancient trade route that connected Europe with China
- **humanism** a way of thought that focuses on humans and their potential for achievement

Impact of Humanism	
Old Thinking	New Thinking

European Society Changes

(pages 429–430)

What helped bring an end to the Middle Ages?

Several key events helped bring an end to feudalism and the Middle Ages. One was the development of unified nations during the 1100s and 1200s. Led by William the Conqueror, the Normans conquered all of England. In France, the nobles who ruled Paris gradually increased their power. They soon ruled much of the land. Eventually, England and France became unified countries ruled by a central government. As a result, individual lords and land owners lost much of their power.

The deadly plague of 1348 also contributed to the end of feudalism. The plague caused a large population decline throughout Europe. This meant that there were fewer serfs to work the land. As a result, the feudal system weakened.

Meanwhile, England and France waged a long battle throughout the 1300s and 1400s known as the Hundred Years' War. The war featured the use of the long-bow. It enabled archers to shoot arrows from long distances. This new weapon made knights and their up-close style of fighting useless.

1. How did the development of nations contribute to the decline of feudalism?

_____

_____

CHAPTER 13

The Expansion of Trade

(pages 430–431)

How did the reopening of the Silk Roads affect Europe?

As the feudal system faded, warfare and invasions gradually grew less frequent. As a result, traders once again felt safe to travel long distances. Because of this, trade began to grow. This led to the reemergence of a strong merchant class and the growth of cities.

As long-distance travel became safer, trade along the Silk Roads also began to grow. The **Silk Roads** were an ancient trade route that connected Europe with China. In 1271, an Italian trader named Marco Polo started a journey along the route. Eventually, he reached China. After 24 years, Polo returned to Italy with tales of riches in Asia. The success of Polo's journey strongly influenced European merchants. Soon they began to increase their trade with Asia. This growth of trade with Asia made Europeans interested in many new goods and ideas.

2. What event brought Europeans in contact with many new goods and ideas?

_____

_____

_____

New Ways of Thinking

(pages 431–433)

What is humanism?

The growth of trade with Asia introduced more Europeans to new goods and ideas. As a result, new ways of thinking spread across Europe. One effect of this was an increased desire for learning. During the Middle Ages, education had declined. This was due mainly to the fact that war and political instability had disrupted society. By the 1200s, people once again wanted to gain knowledge.

To gain greater knowledge, many people turned to the classical teachings of Greece and Rome. Numerous scholars studied the texts from these earlier civilizations. The study of classical texts and ideas led to a movement known as humanism. **Humanism** stressed the study of such classical subjects as history, and literature. The goal of humanism was to create well-rounded individuals. It also encouraged people to achieve all they could in life.

Humanism stressed the importance of the individual. In contrast, medieval thinking placed kings and the church above everything else. Humanist thinkers also stressed the importance of leading a Christian life. But they challenged people to think for themselves and not just accept church orders. They also taught that people could enjoy life and still be good Christians. Before this, people believed they had to avoid life's pleasures to please God. Humanism encouraged people to experiment, explore, and create.

3. How did the ideas of humanism differ from earlier thought?

_____

_____

Lesson 2 The Italian Renaissance

BEFORE YOU READ

In this lesson, you will about how the Renaissance developed in Italy. You will also learn about the artistic achievements of the Italian Renaissance.

AS YOU READ

Use this chart to take notes about the key achievements of the Italian Renaissance.

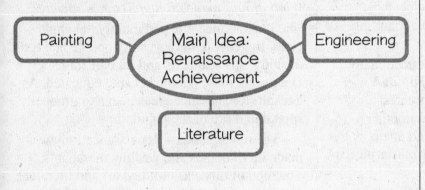

Painting — Main Idea: Renaissance Achievement — Engineering — Literature

The Renaissance Begins in Italy

(pages 435–437)

Why did the Renaissance begin in Italy?

During the late Middle Ages, cities and trade grew in Europe. Europeans also began to focus more on learning and human achievement. All of this led to a movement of great creativity in art and learning. This movement was known as the **Renaissance.** The term "Renaissance" means rebirth. It refers to the rebirth of classical art and learning that took place during this time. The Renaissance lasted from about 1300 to 1600. It began in Italy and then spread to all of Europe.

Several factors helped make Italy the birthplace of the Renaissance. Italy had been the center of the Roman Empire. Because of this, Italian artists and writers were surrounded by classical art and architecture. As a result, they did not have to search far to revive these styles.

Another advantage for Italy was its cities. During the late Middle Ages, trade routes developed between Europe and Asia. Many of these routes went through northern Italy. As a result, many large cities developed in that region. Cities became the main place for exchanging goods and ideas. Because of this, they were great locations for spreading Renaissance ideas.

One of the most important cities of the early Renaissance was Florence. In time, the city became a banking center. The growth of banking brought Florence great wealth.

By the early 1300s, a wealthy merchant class developed in Florence and other Italian cities. Many of its members became powerful leaders. These leaders became **patrons** of the arts. This meant that they encouraged artists to create and supported them financially.

1. What factors helped the Renaissance to start in Italy?

_____

_____

CHAPTER 13

Advances in the Arts

(pages 437–440)

What achievements did Renaissance figures make?

Renaissance writers and painters developed new styles and methods that resulted in unique works. Renaissance artists created works that were more realistic than those of the past. To achieve this, they moved away from a flat, two-dimensional style of painting. Instead, Renaissance artists used a method known as **perspective.** This technique produced the appearance of a three-dimensional painting. As a result, it looked more realistic.

The Italian Renaissance produced many great artists and writers. **Leonardo da Vinci** emerged as one of the period's greatest painters. He also made advances in other subjects, including astronomy and anatomy. As a painter, da Vinci created many masterpieces including the *Mona Lisa.*

Another notable figure of the Renaissance was **Michelangelo.** He was a sculptor who produced many great works. One of his most famous masterpieces was not a sculpture but a huge painting. It was a series of scenes from the Bible painted on the ceiling of the Sistine Chapel in Rome. Other great painters included Raphael, Titian, and Sandro Botticelli.

One of the most important architects of the Renaissance was Filippo Brunelleschi. He is best known for designing and building large domes for churches.

Renaissance writers focused on showing the real life of individuals. An Italian author named Dante Alighieri wrote many poems and nonfiction works. His greatest masterpiece was the long poem *The Divine Comedy.*

Another important author of this era was the Spanish writer Cervantes. His most famous work was the novel *Don Quixote.* In 1513, the writer Niccoló Machiavelli published his most famous work, *The Prince.* This book takes a realistic look at the world of politics.

2. How did Renaissance art differ from works of the past?

_____

_____

Life During the Renaissance

(pages 440–441)

What groups made up Renaissance society?

The Renaissance affected mainly the upper class. In general, only wealthy people had time to study classical texts and humanist ideas. Over time, more people became educated. As a result, Renaissance ideas began to gradually spread to more of the population.

The upper class of Renaissance Italy was made up of nobles and wealthy merchants. The men of this class studied art and literature and other classical subjects. Their goal was to achieve greatness in many areas. Today, we call someone with many talents a "Renaissance man."

Upper-class women also sought to become well-rounded. Many of them received an education. But women gained few social or political rights during the Renaissance. Women of this period stayed mostly at home.

Most people in Renaissance Italy were not wealthy. Many were middle-class citizens who worked as trades people or as merchants. An even larger number of people were poor. These people made up the lower class. Many of them worked as laborers.

3. Why did the Renaissance mainly affect the upper class?

_____

_____

Lesson 3 The Renaissance Spreads

BEFORE YOU READ

In this lesson, you will learn about the spread of Renaissance ideas throughout northern Europe.

AS YOU READ

Use this chart to take notes about the achievements of the Northern Renaissance.

Albrecht Dürer	William Shakespeare	Johann Gutenberg

TERMS & NAMES

- **William Shakespeare** famous English playwright and poet of the Northern Renaissance
- **Elizabethan Age** term referring to rule of Elizabeth I of England
- **Johann Gutenberg** a German who invented the printing press
- **printing press** machine that used movable type to make copies of pages
- **vernacular** the native language of a people

The Renaissance Moves North

(pages 445–446)

Why did the Renaissance spread north?

During the late 1400s, Renaissance ideas began to spread north from Italy to countries such as France, Germany, Spain, and England. There were several reasons why this occurred. One reason was the growth of cities across northern Europe. These cities attracted many merchants, traders, and artists. These groups brought with them the ideas and styles of the Renaissance. The growth of cities also helped to create a wealthy merchant class in the north. These merchants supported numerous artists and writers and encouraged them to create.

The governments of northern Europe also supported the arts. England and France were unified countries ruled by strong monarchs. Many of these rulers took an interest in the arts. As a result, they purchased many paintings. They also provided financial support to many artists and writers.

Interaction between Italian artists and those to the north also helped the Renaissance to spread. In the late 1400s, a war broke out between kingdoms in Italy. Because of this, many Italian artists fled to the safety of northern Europe. There, they shared their new styles and techniques. Artists from northern Europe also traveled to Italy and learned all they could. They then brought Renaissance ideas back to their homelands.

1. How did European monarchs help encourage the Renaissance?

_____

_____

_____

_____

READING STUDY GUIDE CONTINUED

CHAPTER 13

Northern Artists and Writers

(pages 446–448)

How did the Northern and Italian Renaissance differ?

The Northern Renaissance produced a second wave of talented painters, writers, and scholars. They made significant advances in the arts and learning. The Northern Renaissance and the Italian Renaissance differed in several ways. For one thing, Italian scholars valued classical learning. Northern European scholars did not value such learning as much. In addition, northern European artists produced a more realistic, detailed style.

One figure who stood out for his realistic and detailed works was the German artist Albrecht Dürer. Besides paintings, Dürer also created many woodcuts. Jan Van Eyck and Pieter Bruegel the Elder were two great Flemish painters. (Flemish refers to someone who came from a region of northwest Europe called Flanders. Flanders is now in Belgium.) Van Eycks's paintings contain tiny details and bright colors. The paintings of Pieter Bruegel the Elder show everyday scenes. These paintings also show many details.

Talented writers also helped to shape the Northern Renaissance. One of these writers was the Englishman **William Shakespeare.** Many consider him to be the greatest writer who ever lived. Shakespeare became one of the more popular playwrights in England. He wrote comedies, tragedies, and history plays.

Shakespeare wrote during a time in England known as the **Elizabethan Age.** The period was named after Queen Elizabeth I. She ruled from 1558 to 1603. Elizabeth promoted the Renaissance spirit in England.

2. Who were some of the key figures of the Northern Renaissance?

_____

_____

Advances in Science and Technology

(pages 448–450)

How did the Renaissance affect areas outside the arts?

Thinkers made advances in many fields during the Italian and Northern Renaissances. These fields included mathematics, science, and technology.

In mathematics, scholars advanced the study of algebra. Renaissance scientists developed new theories on the universe. Scholars made advances in anatomy, the study of the human body. They also made advances in cartography, or map-making.

Renaissance Europe witnessed many technological advances as well. During the mid-1400s, a German named **Johann Gutenberg** invented the **printing press.** The printing press was a machine that pressed paper against a full tray of inked movable type. The result was an identical copy of the page.

The printing press had a huge impact on European society. Before, printers had to spend months handwriting copies of books. Now, they could produce hundreds of books quickly. The increase of books encouraged more people to learn how to read. It also helped to spread Renaissance ideas more quickly than ever.

The printing press also encouraged more authors to write in the **vernacular,** or their native language. Before this, most authors wrote mainly in Latin. Latin was the language of ancient Rome and the well-educated. Now, many more people wanted to read. As a result, authors wrote to people in their own language. One effect of this was the translation of the Bible into many different languages.

3. How did the printing press help to spread Renaissance ideas?

_____

_____

_____

Chapter 13 The Renaissance

Glossary/After You Read

onset a start; beginning

setback a reverse or change from better to worse

instability a state of not being constant or dependable

insight an ability to see the inner nature of people or things

ideal considered as being the best possible; perfect

masterpiece outstanding piece of work; an artist's greatest work

convey to communicate or represent

famine a tremendous and widespread lack of food

minute extremely small; tiny

dissect to open and expose parts of an animal or human being for scientific examination

Terms & Names

A. Circle the name or term that best completes each sentence.

1. A way of thought that focuses on humans and their potential for achievement is called _____.

   humanism   socialism   rationalism

2. Wealthy individuals who provide financial support to artists are called _____.

   pilgrims   artisans   patrons

3. An artistic technique that produces the appearance of a three-dimensional painting is called _____.

   symbolism   projection   perspective

4. The Silk Roads were an ancient trade route that connected _____.

   France and England   Italy and Switzerland   Europe and Asia

5. The native language of a people is known as the _____.

   prose   vernacular   idiom

B. Write a letter of the name that matches the description.

_____ 6. Italian painter and scientist who painted the Mona Lisa

_____ 7. German who invented the printing press

_____ 8. rule of Elizabeth I of England

_____ 9. Italian artist who painted the Sistine Chapel ceiling

_____ 10. English writer of the northern Renaissance

_____ 11. Italian trader who traveled to China during the late 1200s

a. Elizabethan Age

b. Marco Polo

c. Leonardo da Vinci

d. Michelangelo

e. William Shakespeare

f. Johann Gutenberg

CHAPTER 13

Main Ideas

12. How did Renaissance art differ from the styles of the past?

_____

_____

13. Why did the Renaissance begin in Italy?

_____

_____

14. Why was the Renaissance mainly a movement among the upper class?

_____

_____

15. How did the Renaissance spread to northern Europe?

_____

_____

16. Why did authors during the Renaissance begin to write more in the vernacular?

_____

_____

Thinking Critically

17. Making Inferences How did the teachings of humanism weaken the power of the Church?

_____

_____

_____

18. Forming and Supporting Opinions Do you consider the artistic or scientific achievements of the Renaissance more significant? Why?

_____

_____

_____

Lesson 1 Trouble for the Catholic Church

BEFORE YOU READ

In Chapter 13, you read about the great artists of the Renaissance who worked for the Catholic Church. In this section, you will read about how disagreements over Church practices led to the Reformation.

AS YOU READ

Use a chart like the one below to summarize each of the main sections of Lesson 1.

Section	Summary
The Great Schism	
Criticism of the Church	
Martin Luther confronts the Church	

TERMS & NAMES

- **Great Schism** split that divided the Catholic Church from 1378 until 1417
- **indulgence** the relaxation of earthly penalty for sin
- **Martin Luther** a reformer whose beliefs challenged Church authority and started the reform movement that led to the Reformation
- **Protestants** Christians who broke with the Catholic Church during and after the 1500s
- **Reformation** term used by Protestants to describe the movement of opposition to the Catholic Church

CHAPTER 14

The Great Schism

(pages 461–462)

How did internal differences weaken the Catholic Church?

In the 1300s, the rulers of some nations grew strong enough to force the Church to support their polices. In 1305, the French king used his political power to have Clement V elected pope. Pope Clement V moved the center of Church government from Rome to Avignon, France. After the move, most popes were French. To many Europeans and Church officials it seemed that the French king controlled the pope.

Over time two centers of power developed within the Church. One was in Avignon and the other in Rome. In 1378, each elected different popes. This marked the start of the **Great Schism,** or split within the Catholic Church.

From 1378 until 1417, the Great Schism divided the Church. During this time, both popes claimed power over all Christians. Each excommunicated the other's followers. Christians became confused about which pope had power and authority. The split greatly weakened the Church. It ended in 1414 when the Holy Roman Emperor, ruler of much of central Europe, brought both sides together. At this meeting Church officials forced out the French pope and convinced the Roman pope to resign. In 1417 officials elected a new pope based in Rome.

1. How did the Great Schism weaken the Church?

_____

_____

READING STUDY GUIDE CONTINUED

Criticism of the Church

(pages 462–463)

Why did people begin to question some Church practices?

In the 1300s and 1400s, Church members began to speak out against some Church practices.

Many practices angered reformers. They disliked the way the Church earned and spent its money. Over time, the Church had become a large landowner, owning from one-fifth to one-third of all lands of Europe. Church leaders needed huge sums of money to maintain these lands. Many Europeans, especially those outside of Italy, resented paying taxes to the Church in Rome. They were also angry that the Church paid no taxes on its vast landholdings. Reformers also disliked the way the Church spent its money. Many popes spent large sums on the arts and on themselves.

Reformers also objected to the sale of **indulgences.** An indulgence is the relaxation of earthly penalty for sin. However, people bought indulgences because they believed these indulgences would help them avoid punishment by God in the afterlife. Reformers opposed the idea that someone could buy their way into heaven. Many called on the Church to stress its spiritual values over earthly ones.

During the 1300s and 1400s, several key reformers spoke out against Church practices. In England, priest and philosopher John Wycliffe questioned the pope's right to levy taxes and appoint Church officials without the king's approval. Dutch priest and scholar Desiderius Erasmus criticized Church officials for neglecting Christian values. He also spoke out against reformers for trying to divide the Church. These thinkers influenced reformers in the next century.

2. What Church practices did reformers dislike?

_____

_____

Luther Confronts the Church

(pages 463–465)

Who is credited with beginning the Reformation?

Early Church reformers wanted to improve the Church and work within it. In the early 1500s German-born **Martin Luther** started a movement that openly attacked the Catholic Church. As a young man Luther began to question many traditional beliefs and practices. In 1517, he boldly challenged Church beliefs by listing his ideas in a paper called the Ninety-Five Theses. His ideas included the belief that the Bible was only source of religious truth. He also felt that people did not need clergy to interpret the Bible. He argued that people could be saved only if they had faith in Christ. They could not be saved through good works. These beliefs challenged the Church's authority.

His ideas lead to a fight with the Catholic Church. In 1529 German princes loyal to the Church agreed to oppose Luther's ideas. Prince who supported Luther signed a protest against this agreement. Luther's supporters became known as Protestants. In time all Christians who broke with the Catholic Church during and after the 1500s became known as **Protestants.** They called their movement against the Catholic Church the **Reformation.**

3. What were important ideas from the Reformation?

_____

_____

_____

CHAPTER 14

Lesson 2 Reform and Reaction

BEFORE YOU READ

In this lesson, you will read about how Luther's ideas spread and new Protestant religious groups arose as a result of Reformation.

AS YOU READ

Use a graphic like the one below to record the main idea and supporting details of each section in Lesson 2.

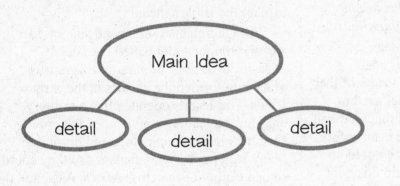

TERMS & NAMES

- **John Calvin** French reformer whose interpretation of the Bible resulted in the Protestant belief system called Calvinism

- **predestination** the belief that people had been chosen for or denied salvation even before they were born

- **St. Ignatius of Loyola** Spanish founder of the religious order called the Society of Jesus, or Jesuits

- **Jesuits** a new religious order founded by the Catholic Church to spread Catholicism

- **Inquisition** a court set up by the Church to investigate people who had strayed from the Catholic faith

CHAPTER 14

Luther's Ideas Spread

(pages 471–472)

What were the some of the effects of Luther's ideas?

Many people learned about Luther's ideas from priests, churchgoers, and merchants. His ideas spread even more quickly through the printing process. As printing became cheaper, it became more widespread. As more Europeans learned to read, printers began to produce the Bible and other works in local languages.

For centuries Bibles were only in Latin. When presses printed Bibles in local languages, people could read and interpret the Bible for themselves. This change threatened the Catholic Church's authority. Church

leaders feared that people would develop their own religious ideas instead of coming to the clergy for religious teaching.

During the 1500s, the spread of Luther's ideas contributed to peasant revolts and religious wars in Europe. Peasants seeking more rights and better economic and social conditions rebelled. Many believed Luther's ideas of individual freedom meant that their protests had God's support. The peasants used Luther's ideas to support their revolts, but few succeeded.

In the mid 1500s religious wars broke out across Europe between Catholics and Protestants. In 1521 Charles V, the Holy Roman Emperor, declared Luther an outlaw. In Germany, many Lutheran princes went to war against Charles. In 1555 Germany's Lutheran and Catholic princes signed a peace treaty ending the fighting.

1. Why did religious division have such a dramatic political impact?

_____

_____

The Reformation Grows

(pages 472–473)

What were some of the different Protestant movements that developed throughout Europe?

Throughout Europe religious thinkers interpreted the Bible differently. French reformer **John Calvin** was a key leader of the Protestant Reformation. Calvin believed in **predestination.** This is the belief that God had chosen certain people to be saved even before they were born. If individuals were not to be saved, there was nothing they could do about it. Christians could not do anything to win salvation. Calvin's religious beliefs, known as Calvinism, attracted many followers.

The Reformation in England took a different path than in the rest of Europe. The English King Henry VIII decided to separate his nation from the Catholic Church after the pope refused to permit him to divorce his wife. Henry established the Church of England, also called the Anglican Church. The Church of England kept most Catholic beliefs, but rejected the power of the pope. English reformer William Tyndale believed the Anglican Church should reject all Catholic beliefs and practices. In England people debated whether to keep most Catholic beliefs or adopt more Protestant reforms.

2. How did the Reformation affect England?

_____

_____

The Counter Reformation

(pages 473–475)

What was the Counter Reformation?

The Catholic Church used many tools to try to stop, or counter, the spread of Protestantism. This effort was called the Counter Reformation. It began with the meeting of the Council of Trent. This was a group of key Church officials who met between 1545 and 1563 to define Catholic beliefs and show how the Catholic faith differed from Protestantism. They ruled that only Church leaders could explain the Bible's meaning.

The Church also set up and supported a new religious order called the Society of Jesus, or Jesuits. Spaniard **St. Ignatius of Loyola** formed the **Jesuits** in the early 1530s. The Jesuits operated like a military unit. Strong leaders commanded the order. Members learned obedience and discipline. Many studied foreign languages so they could spread Catholicism across Africa, Asia, and the Americas.

A third step the Catholic Church took was to establish the **Inquisition.** This was a court that investigated people who had left the Catholic faith. Church officials on the court used threats and torture to get people to confess to sins including that of being Protestant. The Inquisition was used throughout Europe. The most famous court was the Spanish Inquisition.

Church officials also made a list of books including Protestant Bibles they felt were a threat to the Catholic faith. Church officials throughout Europe collected these forbidden books and burned them. The Counter Reformation succeeded in making the Catholic Church stronger.

3. What tools did the Catholic Church use against the spread of Protestantism?

_____

_____

Lesson 3 Expansion of Christianity

BEFORE YOU READ

In this lesson you will learn how European Christians spread their belief systems around the world.

AS YOU READ

As you read Lesson 3, use the diagram below to compare and contrast Protestant and Catholic religious beliefs. List the goals that are different in the circle for Protestant or Catholic and the goals that are shared in the space where the circles overlap.

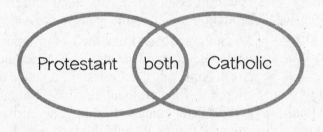

Protestant — both — Catholic

CHAPTER 14

The Impact of Missionaries

(pages 479–480)

What did Protestant and Catholic missionaries do in the 1500s?

In the 1500s the Catholic Church sent church members to places in the Americas and Asia to do religious work called missions. The goal of many missions was to get people who did not share their faith to **convert,** or adopt, their religion. A person who does this work is called a **missionary.** In the 1500s, Catholic missionaries spread their religion around the world. These missions had great success in the Americas but less success in Asia.

Members of the Franciscan, Dominican, and Jesuit religious orders were missionaries for the Catholic Church. The Dominicans were one of the first groups to join Spanish and Portuguese voyages to the Americas.

Until the 1800s, Protestant beliefs were mainly spread by European followers who settled overseas. Most of these Protestants did not try to convert local people to their religion. Some Protestant missionaries did travel to distant lands with the Dutch East India Company. English Puritans organized a religious school to train missionaries and Quakers sought converts overseas.

1. Which faith's missionary efforts met with more success and why?

_____

_____

Responses to Christian Missions

(pages 480–482)

Why were there more Catholic missionaries than Protestant ones?

Catholic missionaries believed Catholicism was open to everyone. Protestants did not seek to spread their beliefs in the same ways. At this time, they did not do much missionary work. Both groups did believe that Christianity should be spread from Europe to other parts of the world.

The spread of Christianity from Europe was linked to European economic growth. Europeans wanted greater trade with eastern Asia. They looked for routes to eastern Asia that bypassed the Muslim empires. Catholic missionaries went with traders. They hoped to win new converts in Asia.

The Jesuits set up missions in India but had little success in South Asia or Japan. Islam attracted many more converts in South Asia at this time. In Japan, the shogun, or military ruler, opposed Christianity. He forced Japanese Christians to give up their religion or be killed. Catholic missionaries won more converts in the Spanish Philippines.

Catholic missionaries had their greatest success in the Americas. France claimed land in North America. Portuguese explorers spread Catholicism to Brazil. By 1700 Catholic Spain controlled most of Central and South America. Catholic missionaries there worked hard to convert Native Americans. Many did become Catholics, but they kept many beliefs of their native religions. Catholicism became the major religion in Central and South America.

English colonists set up the first permanent Protestant settlement in Virginia in 1607. Other English Protestants settled in New England. Over all, however, Catholics controlled more land and gained many more converts than Protestants.

2. Why did Catholic missionaries have more success in the Americas than in Asia?

_____

_____

Legacy of the Reformation

(pages 482–484)

What effects did the Reformation have on Europe?
The Reformation had many long-term effects. Until the Reformation, all Christians in Western Europe belonged to the Catholic Church. By 1700 Western Europe was divided into Catholic and Protestant groups.

After the Reformation religious wars between Catholics and Protestants continued until 1648. At that time, the **Peace of Westphalia** ended most of the fighting and brought some stability to Europe. This agreement marked the permanent division of Western Europe into Catholic and Protestant countries.

France replaced Spain as the most powerful Catholic country. Protestant countries like England, Holland, and Prussia gained power. Through trade and commerce, Protestant countries grew richer. Protestant settlers brought new economic ideas to the Americas.

Some scholars think the Reformation helped democracy develop in Europe and North America. The Protestant practice of church self-government may have brought greater democracy to Europe. The Puritans believed that God had voluntarily entered into a **covenant,** or agreement, with them that allowed them to be saved. This led to the belief that Christians could come together voluntarily to form a church without getting permission from Church leaders. This democratic view of Church membership led to the political belief that ordinary people might also voluntarily form a government.

Some scholars say that covenants also influenced the development of federalism. **Federalism** is the sharing of power between an organization such as a Church or government and its members. This practice may have influenced the framers of the United States Constitution. This important document calls for power sharing between the national government and the states.

3. How did Protestant ideas influence democratic practices?

_____

_____

Chapter 14 The Reformation

Glossary/After You Read

deposed removed from office or power

penalties punishments for crimes or offenses

embody to represent in a visible physical form

mercy to prove or show to be right or just

justify to prove or show to be right or fair

condemned expressed strong feeling or opinion against

awful causing fear, frightening

Counter to act in opposition to; oppose

performed carried out

bypass go around; circumvent

incorporated put into a single larger thing

voluntarily willingly

Terms & Names

A. If the statement is true, write "true" on the line. If it is false, change the underlined word or words to make it true.

_____ **1.** The <u>Great Schism</u> divided Europeans into Protestants and Catholics.

_____ **2.** The belief of <u>Martin Luther</u> that people did not need the clergy to interpret the Bible challenged the authority of the Catholic Church.

_____ **3.** <u>John Calvin</u> led a reform movement to stop the spread of Protestant faiths in Europe.

_____ **4.** The <u>Inquisition</u> was a court set up by the Catholic Church that used fear and torture to get people to confess to such sins as being Protestant.

_____ **5.** The <u>Peace of Westphalia</u> was an agreement that ended most religious wars between European Catholics and Protestants in 1648.

B. Write the letter of the name or term that matches the description.

_____ **6.** Movement of opposition to the Catholic Church

_____ **7.** An agreement

_____ **8.** A pardon for a sin that people could buy

_____ **9.** Spanish founder of the Jesuits

_____ **10.** To change from one religion to another

a. convert

b. indulgence

c. covenant

d. Reformation

e. St. Ignatius of Loyola

Main Ideas

11. How did the Great Schism affect the Church?

_____

_____

12. What Church practices led reformers to speak out in the 1300s and 1400s?

_____

_____

13. How did the spread of Luther's ideas affect European politics?

_____

_____

14. What were two Protestant movements that developed in Europe after the Reformation?

_____

_____

15. How did the Catholic Church work to find new members worldwide?

_____

_____

16. How did economic and political power shift in Europe after the Reformation?

_____

_____

Thinking Critically

17. How did Luther's ideas challenge the authority of Church officials?

_____

_____

18. What legacy of the Reformation had the greatest effect on the people of the United States?

_____

_____

CHAPTER 14

Lesson 1 History of Scientific Thought

BEFORE YOU READ

In this lesson, you will learn about the history of scientific thought.

AS YOU READ

Use this time line to place the main events discussed in this lesson in chronological sequence. This means putting them in order based on the time they happened. Answering the questions at the end of each section will help you complete this task.

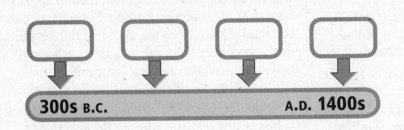

300s B.C.   A.D. 1400s

TERMS & NAMES

- **rationalism** an approach that uses reason, or logical thought, to understand the world
- **geocentric theory** a theory that placed the earth at the center of the universe
- **harmony** the idea of things combining well with each other to form a whole
- **anatomy** the structure of living things
- **dissection** cutting open plants and animals to look at their parts

---

Classical Science

(pages 497–498)

How did classical ideas about astronomy, mathematics, and medicine shape European thought?

Between 600 B.C. and A.D. 200, Greek scientists used an approach called **rationalism.** In this approach, people use reason to expand knowledge. But they do not test their ideas with experiments.

The Greek thinker Aristotle lived from 384 to 322 B.C. He studied the stars and planets in a rational way. His studies led him to develop the **geocentric theory.** This placed the earth at the center of the universe.

An astronomer named Ptolemy lived 500 years after Aristotle. Ptolemy also took a geocentric view of the universe. In addition, he claimed that objects such as the moon and stars move in small orbits of their own. Aristotle's and Ptolemy's view of the universe proved to be wrong. Even so, scientists accepted it for the next 1,400 years.

A Greek mathematician named Pythagoras lived in the 500s B.C. He believed that all things combine in an agreeable way to form the universe. This idea of things combining well with each other to form a whole is known as **harmony.**

About 200 years later, Euclid built on Pythagoras' theories. He studied shapes such as circles and triangles. His work formed the basis of the area of study known as geometry.

The Greeks laid the basis of modern medicine. Hippocrates lived in the 400s b.c. He believed that doctors could identify diseases by studying many cases.

Galen lived in the A.D. 100s. He focused on **anatomy,** or the structure of living things. He gained much knowledge of anatomy through **dissection**—the cutting open of plants and animals to understand their parts.

1. How did the advances made by the Greeks affect medical practices?

_____

_____

_____

Science in the Middle Ages

(pages 498–499)

What role did Muslim scholars play in preserving classical scientific knowledge?

For centuries after Galen's death, little scientific study took place in Europe. European scholars were more interested in studying religion.

Between the mid-700s and mid-1200s, Muslim culture grew. Muslim scholars advanced the learning of classical Greece and other ancient societies.

For example, al-Khwarizmi borrowed the numbering system and zero from Indian scholars. His work resulted in the "Arabic" numbering system. This system is still used in most of the world today.

Classical scientific knowledge spread from the Muslim world to Western Europe. Muslim and Jewish scholars translated classical scientific works from Greek and Arabic into Latin. Christian scholars flocked to Spain to study these works and carried them back to Europe.

The Jewish scholar Maimonides lived in the 1100s. He wrote about religion, science, and medicine. The Jewish scholar Gersonides lived in the 1300s. He made an instrument that measured the distance between objects in the sky. Using it, he discovered that stars were a huge distance from the earth.

Scientific knowledge spread through Europe. As this happened, conflict arose between Christianity and science. Christianity stressed viewing the world through faith. But scientists stressed reason. During the 1200s, Christian scholar Thomas Aquinas tried to combine the two approaches. Reason and faith, he said, both came from God.

2. How did the contributions of Muslims, Jews, and Christians advance knowledge during the Middle Ages?

_____

_____

The Renaissance Leads to New Ideas

(pages 500–501)

How did the Renaissance affect science?

In the mid-1400s, the Byzantine Empire collapsed. Because of this, many Byzantine scholars fled to Italy. They brought with them the knowledge of classical Greek and Roman literature. This literature formed the basis of humanism.

At about the same time, the printing press was invented. This invention helped to spread humanist ideas across Europe. Soon European scholars realized that the classical thinkers did not always agree. As a result, these scholars began to question classical learning.

A revolution in 15th-century art also affected scientists. Artists wanted to show their subjects in a realistic way. To do this, they closely studied humans and animals. Some even dissected human corpses. This study led to a more accurate scientific knowledge of human anatomy.

During the Renaissance, Europeans looked for new routes to Asia. These voyages increased knowledge of Earth's shape, size, and weather. Some of this knowledge challenged classical ideas. For example, Aristotle believed that people could not live at the equator. He thought that the temperature in this region was too high to support human life. Explorers found that the temperatures there were high, but people could live in the region.

3. How did humanism influence learning during the Renaissance?

_____

_____

Lesson 2 The Scientific Revolution

BEFORE YOU READ

In this lesson, you will learn about how the Scientific Revolution developed.

AS YOU READ

Use this diagram to take notes about how the Scientific Revolution. Answering the questions at the end of each section will help you complete this task.

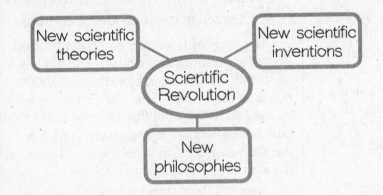

TERMS & NAMES

- **Scientific Revolution** a movement that questioned classical scientific ideas and Christian beliefs
- **heliocentric** a theory that states that the stars, the earth, and other planets revolve around the sun
- **universal gravitation** a theory that claims that gravity acts on all objects throughout the universe
- **scientific method** a way of studying the world based on experiments and observation

New Scientific Theories

(pages 503–504)

What new ideas did scientists develop?

During the late Middle Ages, humanism started to influence scholars. Eventually, they began to question classical scientific ideas and Christian beliefs. This new spirit of questioning the accepted views of the world became known as the **Scientific Revolution.**

In the 1500s, scholars began to look at old scientific beliefs in a different way. A Polish astronomer named Nicolaus Copernicus challenged Ptolemy's geocentric theory. Copernicus reasoned that the stars, Earth, and other planets revolved around the sun. This view is called **heliocentric,** or sun-centered. A German astronomer named Johannes Kepler later used mathematical laws to prove Copernicus's theories.

The Italian scientist Galileo made many scientific advances. These advances challenged classical ideas. For example, some of Galileo's findings supported Copernicus's ideas. But Copernicus's view went against official Church beliefs. As a result, Church leaders forced Galileo to publicly declare that Copernicus's ideas were false.

In the late 1600s, the English scientist Sir Isaac Newton formed a new theory. This theory stated that all physical objects were affected by the same force—gravity. This natural force tends to draw objects toward each other. Newton believed that gravity acts on all objects throughout the universe. Because of this, he called his theory the law of **universal gravitation.**

In 1628, the English physician William Harvey published a work about blood circulation. He accurately described how blood circulates, or moves, through the body.

1. How did Copernicus's view of the universe differ from Ptolemy's?

_____

_____

_____

CHAPTER 15

READING STUDY GUIDE CONTINUED

New Scientific Inventions

(page 505)

What new inventions helped scientists make more precise observations and measurements?

In the 1670s, the Dutchman Anton van Leeuwenhoek built a microscope. Using the instrument, Leeuwenhoek saw tiny moving matter in fluids. This matter is called bacteria.

In the early 1600s, Galileo invented the thermometer. This instrument measures changes in temperature. About 100 years later, the German scientist Gabriel Fahrenheit made the first thermometer that used mercury. He also created the first formal temperature measurement system.

In 1643, Evangelista Torricelli invented the barometer. This instrument measures the pressure of the earth's atmosphere. Later, scientists used the barometer to predict the weather.

2. Why might instruments such as the microscope and the thermometer be useful to scientists?

_____

_____

The Scientific Method

(pages 506–507)

What new ways of viewing the universe did philosophers propose?

Frenchman René Descartes believed in questioning long-held beliefs. He also believed that every idea should be doubted until it had been proved through reason. Descartes argued that God created two realities. The first was physical reality. The other was the mind, or what people think. Descartes claimed that people should use their rational mind to understand the physical world.

The Englishman Sir Francis Bacon also believed in using rational, organized thought. But Bacon did not believe in using abstract reasoning to understand the world. Instead, he felt that scientists should use experiments and observation. This approach, called the **scientific method,** has specific steps:

1. Observing and describing a subject
2. Forming a hypothesis—an unproved belief about the subject
3. Testing the hypothesis in an experiment
4. Interpreting results to draw a conclusion

The ideas of Descartes and Bacon became known as scientific rationalism. The influence of scientific rationalism began to weaken the power of the Church. This started to happen by the 1700s. Why did this happen? Scientific rationalism encouraged people to think for themselves. Before this, people relied more on the views of the Church.

Some political thinkers applied scientific rationalism to government. For example, John Locke believed people have the natural ability to be in charge of their own affairs. He viewed this ability as a natural law or right. Such beliefs led to the development of democracies in nations like the United States.

3. What are the four steps involved in the scientific method?

_____

_____

_____

Lesson 3 The Age of Exploration

BEFORE YOU READ

In Lesson 2, you read how the Scientific Revolution changed the way people looked at the world. In this lesson, you will learn how voyages of exploration greatly changed the European worldview.

AS YOU READ

Use a chart like the one below to write a sentence or two summarizing each of the three main sections. Each summary statement is started for you. Answering the question at the end of each section will help you fill in the chart.

The Age of Exploration
The Portuguese used advances in technology to help . . .
By sailing west across the Atlantic, Columbus . . .
After Columbus' first voyage, several European nations . . .

TERMS & NAMES

- **sponsor** a person who gives money for an undertaking, such as a voyage
- **caravel** a ship with square sails and triangular lateen sails
- **astrolabe** an instrument that measures the angle of the stars above the horizon
- **Treaty of Tordesillas** a treaty between Portugal and Spain that settled which country could claim newly-explored lands
- **circumnavigate** to travel completely around the world

Portugal Leads the Way

(pages 511–512)

How did Portugal find an ocean route to India?

During the Middle Ages, Italian and Muslim merchants controlled overland trade between Europe and Asia. Merchants from other European countries wanted a share of this trade. To do this, these merchants needed to find a sea route to Asia.

Prince Henry, the son of Portugal's king, was a strong supporter of exploration. He set up a school for mapmakers, navigators, and shipbuilders. He also acted as a **sponsor,** or financial backer, of voyages of exploration.

Technological advances helped Portuguese exploration. Shipbuilders in Portugal perfected the **caravel.** This ship was designed for long voyages. Portuguese sailors used a magnetic compass to help them track their direction. The Portuguese also used the **astrolabe.** This instrument helped sailors to find out their ship's latitude.

By 1460, the Portuguese had set up trading posts along Africa's west coast. In 1488, the Portuguese explorer Bartolomeu Dias rounded Africa's southern tip. He then sailed up part of Africa's east coast before returning home. Vasco da Gama extended Dias's route. He sailed east all the way to India in 1498. A few years later, the Portuguese set up a trading post in India.

Sea trade was cheaper than overland trade. As a result, the Portuguese could charge less for spices. Soon Portugal was the leading European power in trade with Asia.

1. How did Portugal become the leading European power in trade with Asia?

_____

_____

CHAPTER 15

READING STUDY GUIDE CONTINUED

Columbus Reaches America

(pages 513–514)

Why did Columbus sail west across the Atlantic, and what did he find?

The Italian navigator Christopher Columbus hoped to find a westward route to Asia. By studying maps, Columbus knew that the earth was round. Because of this, Columbus thought that he could reach Asia sooner if he sailed west. Columbus believed that sailing east would take longer because it involved going around Africa. But Columbus had made a mistake. He thought the earth was only two-thirds as large as it really is.

After six years, Columbus convinced the Spanish monarchs, Ferdinand and Isabella, to sponsor his plan. In August 1492, Columbus left Spain with three caravels and about 90 men. After almost ten weeks at sea, Columbus and his crew reached land. Columbus thought this land was India. He even called the people who greeted him and his men *Indios* (Indians). Once again, he was mistaken. He actually had landed on one of the Bahama Islands. Columbus did not come across any trade goods. Even so, he was still excited at finding what he thought was a route to Asia.

Ferdinand and Isabella did not want Portugal to benefit from Columbus's voyage. They asked the pope to grant them control of all the areas Columbus had visited. In 1493, the pope drew the Line of Demarcation. This was an imaginary line around the world. Spain could claim all lands west of the line. Portugal could claim all land to the east. But Portugal felt that the boundary favored Spain. The **Treaty of Tordesillas** (1494) moved the line more than 800 miles west.

Ferdinand and Isabella sent Columbus on three more journeys west to find mainland India. During these voyages, Columbus found no proof that he was in Asia.

2. What mistakes did Christopher Columbus make?

_____

_____

Exploration After Columbus

(pages 515–517)

Which European countries explored and claimed parts of America?

In 1519, the Spanish sponsored a voyage headed by a Portuguese sailor named Ferdinand Magellan. His goal was to **circumnavigate** the globe. Up to this time, no one had done this feat. During the journey, Magellan and most of his crew were killed. Eventually, the remainder of his crew made it back to Spain. They had successfully traveled around the world.

In the early 1500s, many Spanish explorers came to the Americas in search of gold. Hernán Cortés conquered the rich Aztec Empire in Mexico. Not long after, Francisco Pizarro conquered the Incan Empire in South America. Soon Spain gained control of all of Mexico and Central America and much of South America.

From 1539 to 1542, the Spaniard Hernando de Soto explored the present-day southern United States. In 1540, Francisco Coronado explored the western United States.

The English and French made several attempt to find a short cut to Asia. The Italian sailor John Cabot headed two voyages for the English. He claimed coastal lands in present-day eastern Canada and the United States for England. Between 1534 and 1536, the Frenchman Jacques Cartier traveled up Canada's St. Lawrence River. He claimed the region for France. Cabot and Cartier did not find a short cut to Asia.

Each discovery made by explorers changed the map of the world. Soon mapmakers began to show two new continents. One mapmaker named these continents the "Americas" after Amerigo Vespucci. Vespucci was one of the first to explore and map the coasts of this region.

3. Why did European countries sponsor explorations of the Americas?

_____

_____

CHAPTER 15

Lesson 4 Impact of Exploration

BEFORE YOU READ

In this lesson, you will learn about the results of European exploration in the Americas and beyond.

AS YOU READ

Use this chart to take notes on the impact of European exploration on the world. Answering the questions at the end of each section will help you complete this task.

Results of Exploration	
Causes	Effects
The spread of disease between hemispheres	
The defeat of the Spanish Armada	
The establishment of mercantilism	

TERMS & NAMES

- **Columbian Exchange** the movement of living things between the hemispheres
- **triangular trade** trade exchange between Africa, the Americas, and Europe that involved the shipping of slaves from Africa to the Americas.
- **capitalism** an economic system based on the private ownership of economic resources and the use of these resources to make a profit
- **mercantilism** a theory based on the idea that a nation's power depended on its wealth

The Exchange of Goods and Ideas

(pages 521–523)

What did exploration help to spread?

European exploration resulted in the set up of trade links throughout the world. These trade links increased the exchange of ideas and goods.

The **Columbian Exchange** was the movement of living things (people, plants, animals, and diseases) between the hemispheres. The exchange began after Columbus' voyages to the Americas.

Europeans brought domestic animals, such as horses. In addition, they brought diseases, such as smallpox, to the Americas. Native Americans had no resistance to these diseases. As a result, the diseases killed about 20 million Native Americans. The links among the continents created by the Columbian Exchange resulted in new international trade patterns.

Spanish colonies in Mexico and South America shipped silver from the Americas to Europe and then on to China. In return, such goods as silks, porcelain, and spices went back to Europe.

A different kind of trade developed between the Americas, Europe, and Africa. Sugar cane, which grew well in the West Indies, was shipped to Europe. Slaves from Africa provided the labor needed to produce sugar cane. Cheap manufactured goods from Europe paid for enslaved Africans. This **triangular trade** across the Atlantic went on for more than 300 years.

Culture was also exchanged among continents. The Spanish and Portuguese converted many Native Americans to the Roman Catholic faith. In addition, Europeans often accepted cultural practices from other lands. For example, coffee from Arabia became a popular drink throughout Europe.

1. How did the Columbian Exchange affect world trade patterns?

_____

_____

CHAPTER 15

Rivalry for Colonies

(pages 523–524)

Which European countries competed for colonies?

As world trade increased, European nations competed for colonies overseas. Portugal set up trading posts in Africa, India, and East Asia. It also gained control of Brazil in South America. Spain focused on its silver and gold mining colonies in Peru and Mexico, which brought much wealth to the Spanish.

The Dutch set up a North American colony called New Netherland. But most Dutch colonies were in the East Indies. During the 1600s, the French claimed lands that stretched from Canada down the Mississippi River to the Caribbean. In 1607, English settlers founded Jamestown in Virginia. English Pilgrims settled in Massachusetts in 1620. The pilgrims came to North America to escape religious persecution in England. The English also set up outposts in the Caribbean and India.

English sailors attacked Spanish ships bringing gold from the Americas. This angered King Philip II of Spain. England also supported Protestant subjects who had rebelled against Catholic Spain. In 1588, Philip sent a huge naval force against England. This force was called the Spanish Armada.

The English navy defeated the Spanish Armada. But Spain still received great wealth from its gold and silver mines in the Americas. Because of this, Spain continued to be a leading European power.

2. Which countries had a strong presence in the Americas?

_____

_____

Europe's Economy Changes

(pages 524–526)

How did the events in the Age of Exploration lead to the development of modern capitalism?

The growth of trade and new wealth from the colonies had a major impact on Europe. One of these developments was the growth of **capitalism**—an economic system based on private ownership of economic resources and the use of those resources to make a profit. Merchants who invested in successful colonization and trade ventures made enormous profits. Often, they invested this newly gained wealth in business ventures. Some wealthy investors funded industrial ventures. The chief method of manufacturing at this time was the cottage industry. In this system, merchants provided families with the raw materials to make a product. The merchants then took the finished products to the cities to sell.

Many European nations adopted a new trade policy called **mercantilism.** This policy said that a country's power depended on its wealth. A nation could gain wealth in two ways. First, it could find large deposits of gold and silver. Second, it could obtain gold and silver through selling more goods than it bought.

Some colonies provided the home country with a source of gold and silver. In addition, colonies provided the raw materials to make manufactured goods. Colonies also served as a ready market for these manufactured goods.

By the late 1700s, some people felt that governments played too great a role in the economy. Economists such as Adam Smith argued that the economy should be free of this government interference. Smith's ideas provided the model for the modern U.S. economic system.

3. What economic developments took place in Europe after the Age of Exploration?

_____

_____

Chapter 15 Scientific Revolution and the Age of Exploration

Glossary/After You Read

orbit a path of a heavenly body as it circles around another bodies
agreeable being in harmony
denounce to declare to be wicked or wrong, to condemn
predict to tell about in advance
skeptical doubtful, questioning
feat an achievement that shows skill, strength, or bravery
domestic living in the care of human beings; tame
profitable yielding a monetary return

Terms & Names

A. Circle the name or term that best completes each sentence.

1. The idea of things combining well with each other to form a whole is called _____.

    harmony   anatomy   symphony

2. A way of thinking which states that the stars, the earth, and other planets revolve around the sun is called _____.

    gravitation   geocentric   heliocentric

3. An instrument that measures the angle of the stars above the horizon is called a(n) _____.

    barometer   compass   astrolabe

4. To _____ means to travel completely around the world.

    rendezvous   circumnavigate   voyage

5. An economic system based on the private ownership of economic resources and the use of these resources to make a profit _____.

    democracy   capitalism   socialism

B. Write the letter of the name of a person that matches the description.

_____ 6. a scholar who borrowed Indian numbers to make the Arabic numbering system and developed the subject of algebra

_____ 7. an Italian scientist who was charged with heresy by the Church

_____ 8. a scholar who developed the scientific method

_____ 9. an explorer who reached the Americas in 1492

_____ 10. a Portuguese sailor who led the first voyage around the world

_____ 11. a Polish astronomer who challenged Ptolemy's geocentric theory

a. Galileo

b. Christopher Columbus

c. Ferdinand Magellan

d. Sir Francis Bacon

e. al-Khwarizmi

f. Nicolaus Copernicus

CHAPTER 15

Main Ideas

12. How did Copernicus's view of the universe differ from Ptolemy's view of the universe?

_____

_____

13. What are the steps involved in the scientific method?

_____

_____

14. How did Prince Henry support exploration?

_____

_____

15. How did the triangular trade across the Atlantic develop?

_____

_____

16. How could a nation gain wealth through mercantilism?

_____

_____

Thinking Critically

17. Forming and Supporting Opinions Why do you think individuals, not governments, funded the setting up of most colonies?

_____

_____

_____

18. Making Inferences Why did Columbus believe that he had landed in India in 1492?

_____

_____

_____

CHAPTER 15

Lesson 1 The Enlightenment

BEFORE YOU READ

You have read how scientists questioned old beliefs about nature during the Scientific Revolution. They found new answers through experiment and reason. In this lesson, you will see how the questioning of old beliefs continued in other areas.

AS YOU READ

Use a cluster diagram like the one below to find basic information about the main ideas in Lesson 1.

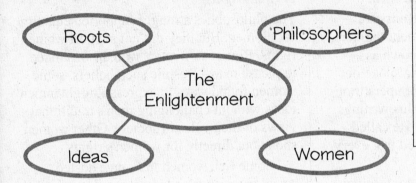

Beginnings of the Enlightenment

(pages 535–536)

Why did the Enlightenment begin?

Scientists began using reason to study nature during the Scientific Revolution. Many philosophers believed they could use reason to understand the political and social world as well. These thinkers called this new way of studying the world the **Enlightenment.** They called it so because they used reasons to enlighten, or shine light on, human concerns. This time was also known as the Age of Reason. The Enlightenment shattered many old beliefs and led to lasting changes in society and government.

The roots of the Enlightenment go back to the Greeks and Romans. Ancient thinkers used observation and reason to understand their world. Their writings also stressed the worth of individuals. Later, the Christian thinkers of the Middle Ages taught that all people were equal in the eyes of God. The Reformation showed that ordinary people had the right to challenge the authority of the Catholic Church. Equality became a key feature of Enlightenment thought.

English philosopher John Locke's writings set the stage for Enlightenment thinkers in the late 1600s. Locke did not believe that kings ruled by authority of God. The power of the government came from the people. It did not come from God or a ruler. People agreed to be governed in return for the government's protection of their **natural rights.** These are rights people are born with such as life, liberty, and property. People have a right to revolt if a ruler fails to protect these rights.

1. What early ideas influenced the Enlightenment?

_____

_____

READING STUDY GUIDE CONTINUED

European Philosophers

(pages 536–537)

Why did European philosophers use reason to criticize social and political institutions?

Thinkers known as **philosophes** believed that people could use reason to understand every aspect of life. These thinkers challenged old beliefs about power. Both Church leaders and absolute monarchs felt threatened by their ideas. Church leaders and kings tried to stop the philosophes from writing or speaking out, but their ideas had a force of their own.

Voltaire, Montesquieu, and Rousseau were three important Enlightenment thinkers. François-Marie Arouet, better known as Voltaire, wrote books in which he spoke out against religious intolerance and superstition in the Church. He was jailed for his writings and later forced to leave France. He called for freedom of speech and insisted that every person had the right to liberty.

Like Locke, Charles-Louis Montesquieu believed that liberty was a natural right. Unlike Locke, he opposed absolute monarchs. He also feared that government could become too powerful. To prevent this, he thought that government should be divided into three separate branches. One would make laws. Another would enforce them. And the third branch would interpret them. Each branch would keep the others from becoming too powerful. His ideas about the separation of powers are part of the U.S. Constitution.

Another thinker, Jean-Jacques Rousseau, argued that democracy was the best form of government in his book The Social Contract. He believed people should form governments that can protect individual rights but also defend rights of the group as a whole. He felt that the people should vote to decide how they were to be governed. He strongly opposed absolute monarchs. He also believed all people are equal. No one should have titles of nobility like duke or prince.

2. What were some important ideas of the philosophes?

_____

_____

_____

Women and the Enlightenment

(pages 538–539)

How did women use reason to argue in favor of equal rights?

The philosophes strongly supported equality for all men. But they did not support women's rights. Rousseau wrote, "woman was made to please man." Despite such beliefs, some women found ways to express Enlightenment ideas without challenging men's traditional views of their roles in society. Other women spoke out directly for women's rights.

Some rich women in France hosted social gatherings called **salons.** They invited important Enlightenment thinkers and artists to these gatherings. Men and women shared equally in discussing ideas.

Other women worked for women's rights by trying to improve education for girls and young women. One of the most important of these women reformers was Mary Wollstonecraft. In 1792, she published *A Vindication of the Rights of Woman.* She believed that women who were well educated would produce enlightened families.

3. How did some wealthy women help spread Enlightenment ideas?

_____

_____

_____

Lesson 2 Democratic Ideas Develop

BEFORE YOU READ

In the last lesson, you read how Enlightenment ideas swept Europe. In this lesson, you will learn how the Enlightenment led some rulers to make reforms and sparked revolution for democratic governments in others.

AS YOU READ

Use a chart like the one below to write a sentence or two summarizing each of the three main sections in Lesson 2.

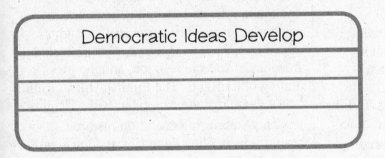

Democratic Ideas Develop

TERMS & NAMES

- **enlightened despot** a ruler who had total control over his people but tried to use power in a just and enlightened way
- **Declaration of Independence** the document in which Britain's American colonies declared independence from Great Britain
- **Declaration of the Rights of Man and of the Citizen** the document issued by the French revolutionary government that list the rights of Frenchmen

---

Enlightened Monarchs Attempt Reforms

(pages 543–544)

Why did some European monarchs make reforms?

A few European monarchs, such as Frederick II of Prussia, Joseph II of Austria, and Catherine the Great of Russia, accepted some Enlightenment political ideas. These rulers were called **enlightened despots.** Despots were rulers who had absolute power. Enlightened despots tried to use their power in a fair and reasonable way. All of these rulers tried to make reforms without giving up their power.

Frederick II of Prussia (present-day northern Germany) is also known as Frederick the Great. He ruled from 1740 to 1786. He made several reforms. He broadened religious toleration, made the legal system more just and allowed more freedom of the press. He also improved education and outlawed torture. But Frederick did not help the serfs—the lowest class in society. Also, he did not help Jews,

who were oppressed in most German states.

Joseph II of Austria ruled from 1780 to 1790. He made more reforms than any other enlightened despot. He freed the serfs and allowed greater freedom of press and worship, even for Jews. Like Frederick, he outlawed torture and reformed the justice system. He ended the death penalty.

Catherine the Great of Russia ruled Russia from 1762 to 1796. Catherine promoted scientific farming methods and developed Russia's natural resources. She opened hospitals and schools, including one for girls, and supported the arts. Catherine planned to end serfdom. But she changed her mind after a serf revolt. She crushed the revolt and gave nobles absolute power.

1. What were two reforms each of the three enlightened despots made?

_____

_____

READING STUDY GUIDE CONTINUED

Democracy in America

(pages 545–546)

How did Enlightenment ideas help spark the American Revolution?

Many Americans thinkers, including Benjamin Franklin and Thomas Jefferson, studied Enlightenment ideas. Both Jefferson and Franklin believed reason was the key to understanding both the natural world and society. Franklin helped open the first lending library in America. Both men worked for freedom of religion. Jefferson founded the University of Virginia.

Colonial leaders used Enlightenment ideas to explain why they opposed British rule. Conflict arose between Britain and its American colonies in the 1770s over taxes imposed by the British. The colonists felt the British government ignored their rights. It did not allow them to be represented in Parliament.

On July 4, 1776, the colonies declared their independence from Great Britain. The **Declaration of Independence** was written by Thomas Jefferson. It reflected his understanding of Enlightenment ideas. The declaration showed Locke's belief in natural law and human rights. It did this when it stated that "all men are created equal." It also expressed Locke's belief that the people have the right to form a new government if the old one does not protect their rights. The declaration built on the democratic principles in the Magna Carta. The Magna Carta was the first document to limit the power of the ruler.

2. How did the Declaration of Independence reflect Enlightenment ideas?

_____

_____

_____

Spread of Democratic Principles

(pages 547–548)

How did Enlightenment ideas continue to influence the United States and the world?

The first government for the new United States was created under the Articles of Confederation. But it proved to be too weak. The federal government did not have enough power. In 1787, the nations best political thinkers and leaders gathered in Philadelphia. They met to write a new plan for government to strengthen the federal government. Their work created the U.S. Constitution. This document reflected many Enlightenment principles, especially in the Bill of Rights added in 1791. The Bill of Rights protected freedom of speech, religion, and the press among other rights. The English Bill of Rights was a model for the American Bill of Rights.

The American Revolution inspired revolutions in other countries and the creation of other democratic governments. The French overthrew their king and created a revolutionary government in 1789. The new government adopted the **Declaration of the Man and of the Citizen.** This document gave French citizens the rights to "liberty, property, security, and resistance to oppression." But women's rights were not included. The Enlightenment ideas that sparked the American and French Revolutions spread widely. They still influence people today who are trying to protect individual rights and freedoms.

3. How did Enlightenment ideas influence the U.S. Constitution?

_____

_____

_____

CHAPTER 16

Chapter 16 The Enlightenment and the Age of Reason

Glossary/After You Read

consent permission

superstition a belief in magic or chance

hostess a woman who receives or entertains guests

outlaw to make unlawful

jolt to surprise or shock suddenly

pursuit an act of seeking

alter to make different, change

Terms & Names

A. If the statement is true, write "true" on the line. If it is false, change the underlined word or words to make it true.

_____ **1.** The <u>Enlightenment</u> belief in the importance of reason started with the thinkers of the Protestant Reformation.

_____ **2.** The philosopher Voltaire was the first to say that government should protect the <u>natural rights</u> of people.

_____ **3.** Joseph II of Austria was an <u>enlightened despot</u> because he abolished serfdom, allowed freedom of press, and made many other reforms.

_____ **4.** The <u>Declaration of Independence</u> reflects the ideas of John Locke and builds on the democratic principles found in the Magna Carta.

_____ **5.** The <u>Declaration of the Rights of Man and of the Citizen</u> gave men and women equal rights.

B. Write the letter of the name or term that matches the description.

_____ **6.** ruler who had absolute power and used it in a just and fair way

_____ **7.** rights that all people have, such as life and liberty

_____ **8.** a social gathering for Enlightenment thinkers in France hosted by wealthy women

_____ **9.** Age of Reason

_____ **10.** group of Enlightenment thinkers who relied on reason to study social problems

a. enlightened despot

b. Enlightenment

c. natural rights

d. salon

e. philosophes

READING STUDY GUIDE CONTINUED

Main Ideas

11. Why is the Enlightenment also called the Age of Reason?

_____

_____

12. What political beliefs of the 1700s did European philosophers criticize?

_____

_____

13. What were two ways women in the 1700s worked for equal rights?

_____

_____

14. How did the reforms of Joseph II reflect Enlightenment ideas?

_____

_____

15. How did Enlightenment ideas help start the American Revolution?

_____

_____

16. In what ways were the American Revolution and French Revolution alike?

_____

_____

Thinking Critically

17. Understanding Continuity and Change Why are Enlightenment ideas important to Americans today?

_____

_____

_____

18. Making Inferences How might absolute monarchs have felt about the Bill of Rights?

_____

_____